PRIDE
IN TRAVEL

T0204291

PRIDE
IN TRAVEL

A TITLE-WINNING SEASON
EXPLORING THE WORLD OF
MANCHESTER CITY

DARRYL WEBSTER

First published by Pitch Publishing, 2014

Pitch Publishing
A2 Yeoman Gate
Yeoman Way
Durrington
BN13 3QZ
www.pitchpublishing.co.uk

A CIP catalogue record is available for this book
from the British Library.

ISBN 978-1-90962-698-0

Typesetting and origination by Pitch Publishing

Printed in Great Britain

CONTENTS

For The Supporters

INTRODUCTION

First Advice

I AM not from Manchester.

Let's get that out of the way. I grew up in East Gwillimbury, Ontario, Canada, a little farming town 45 minutes north of Toronto. My childhood was one of hockey in winter and baseball in summer. In 1994, when I was 17, the World Cup came to North America, the German team training just outside of my small town. An introduction – as it was for so many in our part of the world – was all that was needed to fall in love with the beautiful game.

With the World Cup taking place just once every four years, I quickly needed to find a club team to fuel my new passion. But who should I support and where would I start?

If I were to follow family bloodlines, the choice would be Glasgow Rangers or Hearts. I tried the former on for size for a season or two, but the two-team dominated Scottish league, the aggression, and the religious divide weren't things I was used to, nor did I find them at all appealing.

After Rangers, a girl from Catalonia introduced me to the world of Barcelona. And while I would go on to enjoy watching Barça for many years, the link just wasn't there. Perhaps Barcelona were simply too successful to speak to a person who'd grown up cheering for hockey's most famous underachievers, the Toronto Maple Leafs. Whatever the reason, in both cases, Rangers and Barcelona, something was missing.

In the autumn of 2004, my sister Kimberly made the bold decision to pack up her things at the age of 22, move to Manchester and take a chance on a man she'd fallen in love with. Unable to afford a ticket home during her first Christmas away, she rang me up and asked what gift she might send back to Toronto. An avid collector of jerseys from all sports, I asked Kimmy for a shirt from one of the local clubs. 'Send me City. They wear blue and I look better in blue. And besides, everyone over here has a United shirt,' I told her.

When Christmas day came I tore excitedly into my package, which arrived via Royal Mail. 'How fancy,' I remember thinking. I aggressively separated wrapping paper from gift, revealing my prize, and immediately my excitement turned to disappointment. A jersey of red and black bars stared back at me, no sky blue to be seen.

'Shit, she got it wrong, this looks like United,' was my initial thought. But upon turning the shirt over, I discovered a sleek canal ship, framed majestically by an eagle with three golden stars above its head. The words 'First Advice' were emblazoned across the front, apt words for my first taste of City. I had a lot to learn about my new club, beginning with the significance of these red and black bars.

As I began to follow City – which was difficult for a Canadian in the days of dial-up internet – I began to draw parallels between them and my boyhood hockey club, the Toronto Maple Leafs. For my entire existence, I had supported a losing hockey team, never once seeing them lift a trophy. Toronto's biggest rivals, the Montreal Canadiens, on the other hand, wore red and were the most successful club in hockey history. Sound familiar?

If a gift from my sister got me into City, it was my second trip to the Etihad that cemented my allegiance. My first match was in 2006, when I was nearing the end of a ten-year stretch as a starving indie-musician and found myself in Manchester for my band's first and only tour of Britain. The drummer, myself and my sister's then boyfriend – the man she'd moved to be with – attended a chilly Monday night affair versus Middlesbrough. Richard Dunne smashed one in off his head to bury Middlesbrough by the crushing scoreline of 1-0.

That match, though memorable, wasn't the one that made me City 'til I die. City lost the next one I attended, but it was the manner in which the supporters handled the loss that endeared this unique club to me.

My second game was a 3-0 loss in the pouring rain versus Nottingham Forest. The January night was freezing cold, even by Canadian standards. City didn't even have a decent chance at goal against a club flirting with relegation a full league below them.

Everything about City's performance on that night should have sent me running for a new club. But it was never going to be the players on the pitch who captured this storyteller's imagination. The beating heart of Manchester City Football Club is the supporters; unlike any others on this spinning mass of confusion we call Earth. On that evening I heard a song called 'MCFC OK' and officially fell in love with the passion, the loyalty and the self-deprecating humour that is Manchester City. After years of searching for success, a flailing football club and its supporters' unique ability to laugh at disappointment, finally felt right.

By 2009 I'd had all the rejection I could take from music. After years of ploughing every dollar I had into a slowly sinking ship, it was time to move on. Sensing I was penniless and in need of mental respite, my sister invited me to come and live with her and her boyfriend for a while.

One grey, raining January day, Kim and I decided to walk over to the new stadium for a tour. Despite their rich history, and recent purchase by Abu Dhabi billionaires, City were still Premier League middleweights, and as such there were only four people on the tour: me, my sister and a couple visiting from Australia. Immediately, Kimberly and I recognized our tour guide was a musician. Something about being one yourself, you just know.

This was Chris Nield. He would be our tour guide for the day and in time, one of our very dearest friends. At my leaving do a couple of years later, Chris taught me the lyrics to the song I'd first heard in a loss to Nottingham Forest.

By 2011, feeling refreshed and up for a new challenge, I moved to California to take a series of writing classes offered by the University of California Los Angeles (UCLA). I was there for screenwriting, and only signed up for short-form non-fiction as an elective. My instructor in this class was Norman Kolpas, and just like World Cup '94 and my first electric guitar, he would alter my path in life.

When the course was finished Norman told me I should write a book. Recording albums, attempting film scripts, sure. But a book? What did I know about writing books? I ignored Norman's advice for another year. My life to this point had been a series of abject failures and instead of pushing my artistic limits, I retreated to the safety of my hometown and a job I'd held for many years.

Every aspiring musician needs a day job, and from the time I was 23, mine was managing a local sports shop. When I returned from Los Angeles, the owner and close friend Chris Reilly offered me a chance to buy into the shop with him. I chose safety, and for the next year scarcely wrote a word.

It would take a Manchester City supporters club, located in Toronto, to pull me out of retail purgatory and become the impetus for this book. The more I attended matches at the Toronto supporters club the more I began to realize there was a real story here. I began to believe that Mancunians might be interested in hearing how revered their club and culture was, 3,400 miles across the Atlantic, in Canada's largest city.

I reached out to my old friend Chris Nield; no longer providing the stadium tours, Chris had moved up the City ladder to become one of their social media directors in a social media department very much the envy of world football. I told Chris and his team about a story I wanted to tell, about how big and crazy the supporters club in Toronto had become.

As I researched the story I found myself wondering if there were other international clubs who were this mental for City. Was this happening in other corners of the world? My story on the Toronto supporters club ran over two issues in City's matchday programme, and I didn't want the story to stop there.

When Reilly decided in April that 20 years of being an independent owner meant he couldn't adjust to life with a business partner, it was the final push I needed. I wasn't angry at being let go; running a sports retail shop was never meant to be my life's work. I sold my small portion back to my friend and returned to England for a wedding.

That summer, at my sister's wedding – to the very same man she took a chance on nearly ten years before – with Norman's advice and more than a few bottles of Peroni swirling around in my head, I decided it was time to share my crazy idea with Chris Nield and his fiancée Sophie.

'I want to do a season-long world tour of Manchester City supporter clubs! And I want to write a book about it!' I slurred.

An idea is always at its most vulnerable in that brief moment after your voice has given it life. And the ears that first hear ambitious words are arguably the most important. Chris and Sophie didn't question and they didn't think the idea foolish.

'Get the project started yourself, it will gain momentum. Others will get involved as the idea grows, but get it going now, and don't wait,' was Chris's sage advice.

Which brings us here, to a tiny desk in Toronto, next to a bay window letting in an intruding breeze the maple trees are helpless to stop. It's the evening of 23 July 2013 and I've been sitting here staring at my computer screen for hours now. I've created an online crowd-funding campaign to help get things started. Everything is in place: the PayPal, the banking info, and the YouTube video, all pored over a million times. The only one thing left to do is click 'Go Live'.

The cursor hovers over these two words while a battle rages inside my mind. If I can raise $3,000 that ought to cover me for North America when I factor in that I can stay with friends and fellow Blues along the way. I'll figure out the international stuff as I go; perhaps a sponsor will come on board. Like Chris said, 'Just get it started.'

INTRODUCTION

I must be nuts diving back into the artistic abyss. If I stop now, I'll be okay for money. My debts are under control, my rent is cheap, and I'm sure I could find steady work within the month.

The decision I make next will dictate not only the next year, but undoubtedly many years to come. Can I afford to do this? What if I run out of money? What will I do? Imagine at this age having to call home for money; I'm not sure I could handle that sort of humbling. If I click 'Go Live' then contributions might start coming in. And if contributions start coming in, that will be a promise made and a book will need to be written, a world tour no longer a fantasy but a responsibility. There will be no turning back. Deep breath. Here we go.

Click.

FIRST HALF

Caesar

Vodka (liberal amounts of)

4oz Mott's Clamato Juice

1oz lemon juice

2 dashes Tabasco

Heavy on the Worcestershire Sauce

Rim glass with lime and celery salt

Traditionally garnished with celery

(pickled asparagus at Opera Bob's)

1
TORONTO

The Caesar Opener

It is Monday 19 August, and I've awoken at the crack of dawn to prepare a proper full English breakfast. The sound of morning robins is balanced perfectly against the crackling of frying bacon. The aroma of hope and pork fat sits heavy in the air and brilliantly captures the potential of a new season. After my hearty breakfast I enjoy a hot brew before heading out my front door and taking my first proud step on this journey, a step that takes me, appropriately, east. I'm 3,414 miles west of Manchester but getting closer by the stride.

IN THE days leading up to City's first match of the 2013/2014 campaign, I couldn't help but imagine our journey together beginning this way. It didn't. So let's try this again.

It's 9.30am on 19 August 2013, the occasion of Manchester City's first match of the new campaign. I've woken up late, and if I'm going to make it on time to Opera Bob's 'Caesar Opener' I'll have to skip breakfast, drive instead of walk (which means no beer today) and brew my morning cup at the pub after eating an egg-sandwich-take-away from the Lakeview Diner next door.

For those of you quick with time zones, questioning why I'm rushing out the door at 10am for a 3pm kick-off, the answer is simple: Opera Bob's Public House, the official Toronto supporters club, is holding its first annual Caesar Opener. The Caesar Opener is to be a glorious Monday morning combination of FIFA '13 video-game tournament in which players can only use Manchester City against Manchester City, and consumption of the pre-noon drink of choice here in Canada: the Caesar.

I hop into my modest late-model Nissan, which I still can't afford, parked outside my apartment on Howard Park Avenue. The bright-yellow Toronto parking ticket, which often adorns my vehicle, is fortunately missing this morning, perhaps an omen of a good day ahead.

I'm 3,414 miles west of Manchester and begin this journey by driving eastward. Had I walked, I might have described to you the immaculate front lawns of the residents along Toronto's Dundas Street West, in the heart of what the locals affectionately call Little Portugal. I'll put Portuguese-Canadians head to head with any community on the planet when it comes to pride in their front lawns. My mate Alex Nassar swears he once saw an old Portuguese gentleman vacuuming his grass. I can neither confirm nor deny this account, but it certainly wouldn't surprise me.

Today however, I am driving, battling Monday morning traffic, desperate not to be late. The usually straightforward five-minute drive takes four times that long as I battle my way through taxis, streetcars and slow-moving pedestrians, oblivious to the importance of my getting to Bob's on time.

With only minutes to spare, I arrive one street east of Ossington and park my car next to Roxton Road Park. I used to live at the top of Roxton Road, in the smallest basement apartment into which you could ever fit a kitchen, bathroom and bedroom. I remember having to duck to get in the door and I'm not a tall man. The place was absurdly cheap as the landlord was a good friend, and I *still* had trouble paying the rent most months.

Monday 19 August. City v Newcastle. 3pm kick-off

Somewhere in the neighbourhood of 200 excited steps bring me to 1112 Dundas Street West, the home of Opera Bob's Public House and the official Toronto branch for Manchester City supporters. August in Toronto is hot, sticky-hot, and today is no exception. As I arrive at the pub entrance, sweat drips from my forehead in tidy one-second intervals, on to the notebook held in my left hand, sounding almost like a ticking clock.

Arriving at the door I take a minute to study its lines. The harsh Canadian winters and stifling summers, dramatic expanding and contracting over four years, have carved a unique road map into the heavy and medieval-looking door.

Ross Simnor – the 32-year-old son of a hard-working electrician from Wythenshawe – opened the bar in early 2009 along with his two mates, Will Koplin and Robert Pomakov, the latter an accomplished opera singer (who to this day I've still never actually seen in person) and the inspiration behind the name. In the beginning, Bob's was a mostly empty pub, Ross often by himself, watching City on a lonely bar stool, a single scarf tacked to the wall behind him.

The other two partners didn't know much about football, so Ross's demand that the pub be a place where supporters of his beloved Manchester City congregate was met with little resistance, apart from questioning the $500 a month for a television package allowing the bar to show live soccer matches from England, which nobody other than Ross seemed to be watching.

Will and Bob soon began to ask Ross when exactly these 'soccer people' were going to show up, but even Ross himself wasn't sure. Two months after opening and still without supporters, Ross decided it was time to take action. After thinking long and hard about how to attract more Blues, he devised a plan. He would climb up on a bar stool and pin a second scarf to the wall. Brilliant.

Meanwhile, Ted Masuda and Jimmy Cain were waiting for a nearby music shop to open when they decided to look for a pint to kill some time. Curious, they swung open Opera Bob's ominous wooden door, the Springsteen playing over the speakers convincing them to venture further. A few steps into the pub they discovered a short but broad-shouldered man in his early 30s balanced precariously on a bar stool, carefully pinning a Manchester City scarf to the wall.

'Is this a Manchester City pub?' Teddy asked.

As well as being avid Springsteen fans, Ted and Jimmy were also Blues. After introductions, the three men sat down for a pint and discussed Springsteen's *Nebraska* as it played on in the background. A few pints later and it was The Band's second 'brown' album pouring through the speakers. Eventually the music shop opened and Jimmy and Ted were on their way, but not before promising to return on Saturday for the City match. Opera Bob's supporters club was about to triple in size.

Will and Bob teased Ross, certain he would be stood up on his date with his new football friends. And in some sense they were correct. The club didn't triple in size that Saturday: it quintupled, Jimmy and Ted arriving with fellow Blues 'Big Danny' Dorey and Eric Tokar. Ted's twin brother, Will, who is to this day the club's expert matchday bartender, later followed, forming the foundation for a Manchester City supporters club in Toronto.

In September of 2010 Opera Bob's was granted official status, members enjoying access to certain perks such as the chance to meet guests from the club, former players, attendance at the Player of the Year Awards, and help with organized travel to home and away matches. Four short years after its opening, Ross has transformed Opera Bob's into what is one of the most successful and admired supporters clubs outside of Manchester.

As I step inside the narrow pub, a wave of memories floods my senses. I see the spot where I dropped to the floor in tears when City beat United in the FA Cup semi-final. Walking past the tiny stage to my right, I can still hear Chris Nield and Sophie performing a set of original songs to an adoring pub of Canadians, so tightly packed together that Chris could have walked from stage to bar for a pint without touching the floor. I can recall the exact way my pint tasted, sipping it back slowly, hanging on every word as Stephen Lindsey interviewed his childhood hero Joe Corrigan.

And of course the day no Toronto Blue will forget as long as they live: I remember the chills that ran down my back when Dan Reynolds and Paul Lake marched through Opera Bob's back entrance carrying the Premier League trophy.

At 10am on the nose, I saddle up to the last of a dozen stools at the far end of the bar, just under the Heart of the City award. The Heart of the City was a short-lived but important promotion from Umbro and Manchester City that celebrated supporters clubs around the world, by awarding their pubs a metallic blue moon with the pub name stamped proudly on top. Sitting at the familiar bar, I am already in good company, as the following Blues have beaten me to Bob's:

* Head bartender, twin and dead ringer for Samir Nasri, Bill Masuda.
* Resident expat heartthrob, Rob Kershaw.
* Chris Livesey, who has taken an entire week off from work to facilitate the 3pm Monday afternoon kick-off. He also sports the beginning of what will become, over the course of this season, a glorious white beard.
* David Hampson, who, when I look quizzically at his laptop resting on the bar, tells me he is, 'Working from home today.'

There's no sign of Ross yet, but 'Coach' as he is more commonly known, is a phys. ed. teacher with summers off; there is the likelihood he was into a few beverages last night.

Late waking up, though I may have been, I still managed to rush out the door clutching my lucky 2012 Champions mug complete with tea stains, a few of which have been there since the previous year. Bill quickly puts the kettle on for me, no questions asked; a small detail, but one that makes me feel instantly at home. The markings on the inside of my mug drive my girlfriend mental, but I believe there is a certain measure of character that lies within the stains of one's favourite mug. I like to think Bill notices them as he tosses the bag in. I like to believe he feels the same way I do.

At 10.50am, Bob's big wooden door swings open and floods the cavernous pub with painful morning sunlight. Coach comes bouncing into the pub, the gifted sort of man who can shake off a hangover inside of ten minutes. Coach hooks up his PlayStation to a giant theatre screen and the first annual Opera Bob's Caesar Opener begins.

When the clock strikes 11am, the time you can legally begin serving alcohol in Ontario, Bill starts preparing the Caesars and Rob Kershaw's home-kit Blues kick off against the away-kitted City side of Jason Nebelung.

The Caesar is a Canadian staple. It is a drink we annually consume by the millions, but that remains virtually unknown outside of our borders – and perhaps that is what we like most about it.

The rest of the world might tell you it's simply a Bloody Mary with clam juice, but don't ever describe it this way to a Canadian.

The next four hours see a group of ten grown men wage civil war on one another on a Monday afternoon when most of our countrymen are hard at work. I even jump in for a quick match and get shelled 8-1 by Kershaw's Blues. It was 1-1 for a time, but when I over-celebrate my Balotelli equalizer by running around the pub airplane-style, Rob quickly reminds me who's boss, and pours in another seven on the trot.

2.23pm Eastern Standard Time, we're 37 minutes from the start of the 2013/2014 campaign and the Toronto Blues begin to arrive, seemingly by the streetcar load. I'm so excited I can barely write in my John Rylands notebook. It has been an uneventful summer without footy – apart from my sister's wedding in Oxfordshire, of course – but aside from that, summer was as summer nearly always is for me: hot and dull. I don't care for the heat and have no interest in tennis.

The chairman of Toronto's official supporters club is Dan Reynolds. Months from now, on a cold and rainy night in Manchester, he will tell me his plans to move to Tel Aviv, leaving the Toronto Blues in need of a new chairman. But on this day, Dan Reynolds is still very much our leader.

'Thought you said you weren't drinking today,' I say.

'I skipped work for this, may as well get drunk.'

'You want that off the record?' I joke.

'Oh, that is very much *on* the record sir!'

'How did you become a Blue?' will become the question I ask people the most in the coming year, as well as the most common question asked of me. Perhaps it is the excitement of opening day, or the fact that Dan and I have felt like old friends since the day we met, but as I stand beside him on this humid August day in 2013, I am entirely unaware of how he found City. For now, Dan is simply a friend and our chairman, anxiously clutching his third pint of stout.

At 2.31pm, the nearly-full pub erupts in unison, 'Woody!' Mark Wood has just entered the pub. Originally from Reddish, Woody, a season ticket holder for nearly 20 years, was offered a job in Toronto he simply couldn't pass up, and in the summer of 2012 he moved his wife and two daughters to Toronto. Woody, Jeanette, Charlotte and Hannah have adored their first year in Canada and it looks like they – much to our country's benefit – are here to stay. Woody's new job at our nation's largest newspaper is very much of the Monday to Friday variety and it begs the question,

'Woody, how'd you get work off?'

'Told them I had an immigration meeting, pal,' replies Woody with his signature wry smile and raised eyebrow.

Funny, Woody is the third expat through the door with an immigration meeting today.

Woody orders his customary spiced rum with ginger ale and lime wedge before turning to me and asking, 'How have you been, *amore*?'

There's a small chance you're wondering why a 43-year-old married father of two refers to me as *amore*. It's a slightly embarrassing story, but one worthy of a quick telling.

On 13 May 2013 I drove 45 minutes north to my parents' house to watch the most important Toronto Maple Leafs hockey game there had been in eight years. As I sat down to watch the game with my father – this game was far too big to watch with anyone else – my phone began to light up. My traditional hockey friends are, like me, too nervous to be texting back and forth during such a huge game. So who could be sending me so many messages at such an important time?

As it turns out, there were two offenders. The first was my girlfriend, Jess, who was away at university in Montreal. Jess despises sports and was firing off a million texts at once, likely knowing there was a big game on and wanting to test which I valued more, our relationship or a hockey match.

The other offender, you've likely guessed, was Woody. Woody decided to get into hockey when he moved here and loved it from the first drop of blood, but he has trouble understanding the myriad rules of professional sport's fastest game. So there I was, trying to enjoy Toronto's biggest match in eight years with my dad and my phone is receiving five texts a minute from Jess and another ten from Woody. I figured I could get Jess off my back by composing the sweetest, most nauseating text imaginable. Something that professes my undying love, compliments her eyes and praises her hair – Colombian women are suckers for a good hair compliment.

Quickly, during a commercial break I tap away a muddled list of 'I love you' messages and 'you mean the world to me' and of course, 'Your hair is softer than silk.' Admittedly, not my best work, but this was an elimination hockey game – lose and we're finished!

And I only had a two-minute commercial break to work with. I finished off the message with some of those nauseating hearts and smiling faces, and smiling faces with hearts in the eyes and pushed send. And by now I'm sure you've figured out to whom it was sent. Woody simply replied with one simple word, 'Amore!'

Safe to say he'll never let me live that one down.

By the time Jesus walks through the door, the narrow pub is already pushing its capacity. Dan Reynolds leaps to his feet and quickly welcomes the new arrivals, a vacationing family from Chadderton, their youngest wearing the kit of our brand-new signing Jesus Navas. Danny is a savant at making new people feel welcome at Opera Bob's; you couldn't dream of a better chairman.

At 2.45pm the new season is minutes away. I order myself a pint of the local King Vienna and a meat pie – if this isn't heaven, it's damn close. As I savour my first pint of what will be a record-breaking number this season, a glass jar behind the bar catches my attention. I haven't seen it before; a note taped to its front reads 'C-word jar'. In England, should the appropriate moment call for it, the 'C-word' in question isn't entirely unheard of and given the right circumstances (referee grants seven minutes of added time) is even somewhat forgivable.

But this word in North America carries a little more weight; one simply does *not* say this word in mixed company without reprisal. Few words are more reviled here, and so at Opera Bob's, should the word be uttered, the offending supporter must pay a one-dollar fine to the jar in question. This isn't Coach's policy, rather that of his wife, Brittani. And the lads here know better than to question Brit. Dropping the C-word at Opera Bob's is going to cost you a buck; pay up and say sorry.

Before the match begins, City honour their former keeper Bert Trautmann, a man who famously played and won the 1956 FA Cup Final with a broken neck. The current squad all wear Trautmann kits and the Opera Bob's faithful belt out 'There's only one Bert Trautmann'. From there the Bob's Blues launch into 'There's only three Samir Nasris,' sung because, as mentioned, Bill Masuda and his twin brother, Ted, and their eldest brother Ed, all bear a striking resemblance to City's number eight.

The 2013/2014 campaign, one which will change my life forever, finally kicks off, and before I'm two bites into my meat pie, David Silva heads a deflected Edin Dzeko cross into the back of the Magpies' net and Bob's goes absolutely mental. From their usual seats just in front of the giant pull-down theatre screen, I watch Coach and Woody share a particularly exuberant hug, the bastards having just won our first-goal-pool. At 5/1 on Silva, Woody is $25 richer, and due for a few more spiced rums.

Up 2-0 at the half, thanks to Sergio Aguero, City are rolling and the locals are buzzing. I grab myself a cup of tea and it's time to talk with Jesus. Andrew and Wendy Woods were married 19 years ago today. They've come to Toronto to celebrate their anniversary and they've brought along with them daughter Ellie and son Alexander to visit family friends and local restaurateurs Alexandra and Craig Hutchinson. Alexandra – who admits she has never been to watch a footy match in a pub or otherwise – tells me she is quickly falling in love with City, and I'm not the least bit surprised. The atmosphere on this Monday afternoon is absolutely on form, and I always say a person only needs an introduction to City culture to become forever hooked. Forty-five minutes in, Alexandra is hooked.

A few minutes into our chat I begin to see the sea of sky-blue jerseys part; it's the youngest of our new arrivals from Chadderton, Alexander, he of the new Jesus Navas kit. Weaving through the packed Toronto pub, a Coke in his hand, and even at eight years old, that confident Mancunian swagger, he saunters up to the table where I am interviewing his parents and tells me in no short order, 'I'm going to be famous. I'll wear number ten for City and drive a Bugatti Veyron!'

Alexander next informs the table City will take this match 5-0 and like that, he's gone, back into the ocean of City blue, high-fives and fist-bumps galore, navigating the strange Canadian pub-waters as though he was born to them. He is the star of the show today and Opera Bob's wouldn't have it any other way.

EN-RI-CO!
Whoa-oh,
En-ri-co, whoa oh-oh-oh,
He comes from Italy,
To cheer for Man City!

Our singing section, better known as 'The Pit', led by Marty Von Wuthenau, Jason Nebelung and Dan Rouse, belts out a pub favourite when Enrico Galati finally arrives on the scene. Manager at Toronto's favourite independent grocer, Fiesta Farms, Enrico is one of Opera Bob's original Blues, and even though Mancini has left us, the pub continues to serenade Enrico with his personal anthem. In a season where so much is about to change, it's good to know some things never will.

The second half kicks off against a ten-man Newcastle side with an impossible hill to climb. The remaining 45 minutes are simply a party; pints flow, endless hugs are exchanged and true friendship, both new and old, rules the day. City are back and it's a dream start to the campaign. City look so dominant today, I catch myself wondering if this journey will see a City loss at all. Could this be our version of the invincibles? That's how impressive our lads looked today in their debut under a new Chilean leader, manager Manuel Pellegrini.

Toronto

When I finally leave, eight hours after arriving, I find Woody outside holding court with some more new arrivals to the Toronto club. They're Canadian Blues and hang on Woody's every heavily accented word. Woody regales the three men nearly half his age with tales of matches in places they've never heard of, much less been to: Macclesfield, Tranmere, Chesterfield. If I know Woody, he is just about at the part of his story where in 1997 he and some mate of his called Tim Bramley started up a supporters branch called the Reddish Blues. The Reddish Blues always sounded like a funny name to me, but more on that gang later.

I say a quick goodbye to my *amore* and walk back down Dundas Street towards Roxton Road, not really having any idea if what I am about to get myself into is a good idea or just completely crazy, another soldier standing at useless attention in my long line of failed ideas. My hometown was always going to be an easy, affordable and welcoming start, but now I must begin travelling to places I've never been, soliciting stories from complete strangers with the hopes they'll give up some of their most personal experiences.

I am crazy, I'm certain of it.

Just steps away from the pub and already the bliss of a 4-0 win has given way to anxiety and doubt. Then, in the distance, I hear Woody. His voice carries further than the others as I hear him describe me in three simple words, 'Proper Blue, him.'

And with that endorsement I'm off to Washington, DC with my chin up. If a born-and-raised Blue from Reddish believes in me, perhaps my idea stands a chance. Perhaps I can get people to talk.

Perhaps one of my crazy ideas might just be, at long last, a good one.

CAPITAL CITY BLUES

2
WASHINGTON, DC

The Legend of Jonny Danish

AIR CANADA flight 7354 to Reagan National Airport begins ominously as a stocky French-Canadian flight attendant tosses an older Asian gentleman out of first class. Between her thick *Québécois* accent and his lack of any English, the situation appears to be more than just lost in translation. I for one can't figure out why this gentleman sent a woman, who appears to be his wife, back to coach while he attempts to claim a single seat in first class. Whatever the case, our flight attendant is not having it; this guy is getting chucked out of first class and it's all going down, nearly on my lap, in the first row of coach, right on the dividing line between wealthy and cattle. Funnily enough, the first-class seat in dispute was nearly mine.

The previous night I'd been out for the stag do of Bryan Andrachuk, a close friend from childhood. I took it relatively easy: five tall cans and home by midnight. Five tall cans, however, is just nearly the amount I require to make ill-advised purchases, such as a beef patty from the corner shop, a $20 scratch-ticket, or let's say, an upgrade to first class on a flight to Washington. When I got back to my apartment there was a check-in email from the airline with what seemed a very reasonable offer of $169 to upgrade to first class.

I've never flown first class before, but I was nearly drunk enough to pull the trigger on an awful idea. Six beers and I'd have been in the front section of this plane, but five beers instead put me nicely to sleep and here I sit, in the first row of coach with a perfect view of the action.

'Sir, don't push me! Do *not* put your hands on me!' shouts the flight attendant.

The man, English-speaking or not, finally appears to grasp the fact he is extremely close to being air-marshalled off this flight and retreats to the back of coach with a woman I suspect is his very lonely wife.

Moments later, a well-tailored man in his 50s strolls on to the plane, smiles hello and claims the empty seat in first class. The Chinese gentleman wasn't getting tossed out of *his* first class seat, he never had one to begin with! He was merely a chancer taking a swing; fair play to him. The rest of the flight proves uneventful. I'm flanked by two muppets wearing sandals – how sandals are legal on flights and hair gel isn't, I'll never know. The usually off-putting in-flight air filters through the cabin and feels strangely soothing on my hangover. I land one hour later in Washington feeling refreshed and ready to go, two tins of lager having assisted nicely.

It is a special day to arrive in the American capital, the 50th anniversary weekend of the march on Washington led by the Rev. Martin Luther King. On this very weekend in 1963, my grandfather made the journey down from Canada to march in solidarity with his American sisters and brothers for racial equality and workers' rights. Following in his footsteps all these years later makes me wish he were here to share it with.

The ride to my hotel reveals the curious fact that DC's subway is carpeted. I can't imagine this is a good thing when you carry drunken American football fans to and from the match and I certainly don't envy the custodians of DC's Metro trains; hopefully they have a good deal of bleach at the ready.

Today is 24 August and Manchester City don't play Cardiff City until tomorrow morning, so I have some time to check out the first away city of many on my journey. It's Saturday, yet the streets are empty and everything appears closed. I find Pennsylvania Avenue busier and by the time I reach the White House, the city is alive! A large protest group has gathered, the subject of their anger being the recent acquittal of a Florida man who shot an unarmed teenager named Trayvon Martin. The impassioned crowd chant 'Tray-von' followed by 'Mar-tin' never tiring, only getting louder by the minute.

I followed a good deal of the Trayvon Martin trial and am on the side of the protesters: I believe his killer should be in prison. I want to join the protest, but I've never been in a crowd of so many angry people, not even at the fiercest of derbies; it's a different kind of anger than sporting anger, it is a much more noble angst. Nervously, I wade into the gathering – made even more surreal by the contrasting Midwestern Americans wearing khaki shorts, whizzing past on Segways on a chaperoned tour of DC – snap a few pictures, and decide it's time to move on. Looking back, I wish I'd done more. I wish I had stayed and lent my voice, but I didn't. I should have stayed longer.

Later, when I return to the National Mall, most people have cleared out and gone home and again I feel I've missed something I should have experienced. With most of the people gone, I do, however, have easy access to the steps of the Lincoln Memorial and stand on the exact spot where Dr King gave his famous 'I have a dream' speech 50 years earlier.

I take time to gaze out over the nearly mile-long reflecting pool stretching to the Washington Monument and imagine my grandfather doing the same, before concluding he would have done differently. My grandfather wouldn't have taken a nap, nor skipped the protest in favour of lunch. I should have stayed with the Trayvon protesters a little longer. I should have tried to make it to the National Mall by early afternoon. But I didn't and I regret this. I will let this be a lesson to me: When travelling, never choose the easy option. March, protest, sing, eat, drink, meet new people at all costs and always venture a little outside your comfort zone.

Sunday 25 August. Cardiff City v City. 11am kick-off

The morning of the match arrives and after a full breakfast of two eggs over-easy, bacon and a side of home fries – home fries are like chips, but far more acceptable in the morning – I'm ready for some footy! Moreover, I'm excited to make some new friends and find out how the hell an official Manchester City supporters club came to exist just a ten-minute walk from the White House.

I walk the five short minutes from my hotel to my first away match at Lucky Bar, 1221 Connecticut Ave. My stomach is tied in knots; I wonder if Manuel Pellegrini is this nervous ahead of his first away match. I knew Toronto would be great; Toronto is home, home is familiar and familiar is comfortable. Now this crazy idea of mine is moments away from becoming a reality and as many of us do when an idea transitions from planning to implementation, I'm shitting it just a little.

From the corner of Connecticut and North Street Northwest, I can see Lucky Bar, its simple dark-green bunting looking more like the entrance to a Manhattan apartment building than a sports bar. I walk in the front entrance, about 15 minutes before kick-off, and discover a completely empty bar, and when I say empty, I mean that I don't even see a bartender. Terrific, Webster, I think to myself. *Pride in Travel: A Lonely Man's Journey Exploring Empty American Pubs.* My greatest fear realized, two cities in.

But a few more investigative steps past a small bar with hundreds of different soccer scarves brings me to a back room and to my relief it already holds a good number of sky-blue-clad patrons. Lucky Bar has a roughly 1,300-square-foot back room with a large flat screen on each wall, a giant pull-down theatre screen and its own bar along the side. It smells exactly like every pub I've ever experienced in morning hours, that welcoming aroma of sickness and bleach. If I closed my eyes, I'd swear I was back in Toronto loading my band's equipment into the Horseshoe Tavern.

The first person to introduce himself is an imposing figure named Moritz Reiter. A former US airman and veteran of the Persian Gulf War, Moritz keeps his head shaved, wears a goatee, and his broad shoulders fill every stitch of his City home kit. In the unlikely event a gang of unruly Cardiff City supporters were to waltz in to Lucky Bar, Moritz's is the table you'd want to be sitting at.

'Are you Darryl?' Moritz asks, just barely above the volume of a polite whisper.

I tell him I am and he immediately invites me to sit at his table.

Moritz was born and raised in New York and grew up loving the Cosmos of Pele and Franz Beckenbauer. But when the league folded in 1984, he was left with a love of soccer and no club to support.

'A new guy named Tom, with a strange accent, moved into my neighbourhood and for whatever reason my friends and I just loved talking to him. Then one day in the summer we were kicking a ball around on the block and he started talking to us about football. I told him I used to go see the New York Cosmos, but that it was over now and I didn't have any team to cheer for. He quickly said, "Have you never heard of Manchester United?" I said, yeah, they sound familiar, should I root for them? And he told me, "Never in a million years! You should be supporting the greatest club in the world, Manchester City Football Club." Then he ran inside and got his scarf.'

Joining Moritz at the table are Timo, Andy LaGow, Pat Weitzel and Tim Kirby. Originally from Salford, Tim is somewhat surprisingly one of only a few expats in a room filled with American City supporters. If Moritz is quiet and reserved, six-year-old Timo is his polar opposite. Boundless energy and two questions for every answer you can throw at him. I feel like I'm in that scene from *Uncle Buck* when Macaulay Culkin is peppering my fellow countryman John Candy with 20 questions, my favourite of which comes when Timo twists a black cocktail straw to emulate his father's goatee and asks, 'Who am I?'

Moritz informs me that he and Tim are the 'senior citizens' of the Capital City Blues, by virtue of both being in their 40s, but neither of the men look 40 and Tim doesn't appear at all fond of the nickname. When Johnny Marr rolled into town recently to play the 9:30 Club, Moritz and Tim were there with City scarves held high.

'Johnny pointed his guitar like a rifle and aimed it straight at us!' Tim states proudly.

Andy LaGow designed the Capital City Blues' logo, the United States Capitol building in blue, with the Manchester City ship in the centre of its iconic dome. It remains one of the sharpest supporters club logos I'll see on this journey. I ask Andy how he got into City and everyone at the table laughs, even Andy. Andy, who came to DC as he tells me, 'by way of Nebraska and Oregon, and oh yeah, by way of New York, too!'

Andy admits he is entirely new to footy and has little clue what's happening on the pitch. But he loves the atmosphere, and thanks to the Capital City Blues he is learning quickly, in what I can already tell is a welcoming, knowledgeable and supportive place to do so.

Pat Weitzel was one of the earliest Capital City Blues, who themselves only officially began congregating at Lucky Bar the previous season. It's heartening to be at a club so young and feel the potential, knowing it will grow exponentially in years to come.

The energy is surprising, the innocence genuine. It reminds me of Opera Bob's three or four years ago, and ten minutes into my visit I already know this club has some special days – and indeed years – ahead.

Just as I'm about to get up and investigate the bar, seemingly out of nowhere, a man in giant blue mirrored aviator sunglasses and an instructional T-shirt on how to do City's favourite dance, The Poznan, enters my field of vision. He extends his right hand and we shake. 'I'm Jonny Danish,' he says.

The following information storms from Jonny's lips in less than three seconds, 'I've got numbers for you.

Numbers for LA and numbers for San Francisco, when you get out there. The San Fran guy and the LA guy are actually the same guy but I'm gonna get you a few numbers anyways. And email addresses, what's your email address? Actually hang on, don't tell me that yet, I'll be back, I've gotta do a shot.'

Before I can ask if it's Danish the citizen or the delicious pastry, Jonny is off and I'm left to wonder if any of that really just happened.

It's 10.55am and I ask the table, 'When is first call around here?'

They struggle to understand the question. Pat knows what I mean, but says he's only heard of such prohibitions in Tennessee, and assures me they've been served here as early as seven in the morning. I put down my notebook and decide it's time for *Pride In Travel*'s first away pint. There has been a phenomenal rejuvenation of the craft beer scene in the United States over the past ten years and I'm excited to try something new and local. I walk up to the small back-room bar, passing by a still sunglasses-clad Jonny Danish as he heads the other way, a shot of what looks like whisky in one hand and a bottle of beer in the other. I can't be sure, but I swear he is humming the tune from *Knight Rider.*

I investigate the dozen or so tap handles and one immediately jumps out. DC Solidarity Brau, its bright-green handle like a glowing beacon shining directly into my eyes. The lone bartender arrives and asks, 'What it'll be?' in the manner we all expect from American barkeeps.

Looking back on this moment, I still cannot believe the subsequent words from my stupid mouth.

'Yeah, this DC Solidarity Brau, is that local?' asks the tourist moron.

I quickly realize the idiocy spilling from my mouth and desperately try to tuck the words back in, like a bag of Skittles opened upside down. But it's too late, I've said it, and bartenders are rightfully low on patience on a good day, but this question at 11am on a Sunday? Alright Washington, let me have it.

The bartender delivers a well deserved 'You gotta be kidding me' stare before simply muttering 'yeah'. Uncomfortable pause. 'It's local.'

The man beside me wearing a DC United cap is even less forgiving. 'Hey, you know what DC stands for?' He asks.

'No?' I cringe and wait for his answer.

'Dumb question!'

The bartender enjoys the jab and has a good laugh at my expense; I laugh, too, and both men seem to appreciate the fact I take the teasing good-naturedly. I'm starting to like Lucky Bar.

I take my DC Brau – which is excellent, by the way – back to my table, just in time for kick-off. The back room has filled up to about 30 Blues now and it's a good turnout for a Sunday morning versus Cardiff City in August. The volume of the Cardiff supporters coming through the speakers impresses everyone; it feels like we're hearing them all the way from South Wales and they certainly sound up for a fight today. Too bad nobody told them we're Super City from Maine Road and they haven't got a chance.

A few minutes into the match Matthew Eide, chairman of the Capital City Blues, finally arrives at Lucky Bar. By this point, three or four of the lads have told me varying accounts of how the Capital City Blues began, but they all seem to agree that Matthew Eide, if not the man who directly started the club, is certainly the one who got them organized.

There is a buzz about Matthew today and it has something to do with the yellow envelope tucked under his arm with large block-letter printing scrawled across its front. I know this package and I recognize the handwriting. 'Just arrived from Mother. It's our membership cards!' Matthews says, absolutely beaming. I know you can't sell membership cards without being official.

'Are you guys official now?' I ask.

'Yep! This is our first year,' Matthew answers proudly.

I like Matthew from the first moment he sits down. He reminds me of a younger, trimmer version of the drummer from Weezer.

As Matthew begins telling me how he moved to DC after a break-up with a girl in Arlington, I am floored by how he and Toronto Blue Chris Harris, the man who secured Opera Bob's OSC status in 2010, are alike – a great compliment as Chris Harris is a true gem, a proper Opera Bob's legend.

Matthew explains to me that he is originally from Minnesota and things begin to make a lot of sense. To me there is a Canadian-ness about Minnesotans, or perhaps we have a Minnesotan-ness about us. Either way, of the few great Minnesotans I've had the pleasure of knowing, they all feel like compatriots. I tell Matthew this and he offers his theory, 'I think it's because we both understand truly harsh winters.'

I couldn't agree more.

As Matthew continues telling me about the early days of the club, suddenly the DC hat-wearing gentleman, he of the 'dumb question' remark, catches my eye. He has ordered the single largest – American version of – a full English breakfast I have ever seen in my life. I'm listening to Matthew and staring in astonishment at a mountain of food no human could possibly finish.

As you might imagine, Washington is a hub of networking, filled with lobbyists, politicians and, of course, foreign embassies. For the opening day match against Newcastle, the Capital City Blues entertained members of the UAE embassy and once, at a business breakfast, Matthew even met City's chairman Khaldoon Al Mubarak.

'I had no business being there,' Matthew explains. 'It was all Boeing executives, CEOs, you know these types. A friend of mine knew I was chairman of the Capital City Blues and invited me along. After the breakfast and a bunch of speeches, my friend asked if I wanted to meet Mubarak. I was nervous as hell, but I said sure. Standing there in line I could hear CEO after CEO speaking with him and he never broke the demeanour of a very serious businessman.'

Matthew gets into character and gives it his best Khaldoon Al Mubarak impression. 'Yes, yes. Very interesting. I'd like to discuss that further, we are definitely very interested.'

As I've never met Mubarak, I'll have to assume Matthew's impression is bang on. He continues with his story, 'So it's my turn to meet him, and I stick out my hand and all I can say is, "Hi I'm Matthew Eide, chairman of the local Manchester City supporters club here in DC." Instantly his eyes lit up and his entire demeanour changed. He wanted to know all about our club and was desperate to talk football! I could tell this was a man who truly cared about the game and loved City.'

Matt takes a sip of his Bloody Mary, 'I was never sure how I felt about the new ownership group before that day, but I'm convinced now. At their core, they are football fans, City fans, and I feel absolutely confident with them in charge.' Matthew thinks for another moment and with a smile he tells me, 'You know, I asked him if there was anything I could do and he told me, "Triple the size of your club." I gulped, because I think he was serious!'

Before getting up to make his rounds, Matthew asks if I've met the other Capital City Blues and I tell him that for the most part I have. Just before leaving he tips me off that the club does have one official nutter, 'There's a guy here named Jonny Danish, great guy but a bit crazy. You see that table over there?' Matthew points out a large horseshoe-shaped table in an elevated booth.

'Jonny stood up on that table during a match once. I begged him not to, but he wouldn't listen. Ended up flipping the entire thing, completely full of pints and breakfasts.'

Matthew heads off to say hello to the rest of the gang and right on stage cue, who should appear to fill his empty seat?

In the same moment that Matthew leaves the table, Jonny arrives back, standing in front of me, holding a model of cellphone no one has used in at least a dozen years in one hand and a bottle of Budweiser in the other.

'You know how I became a Blue?' Jonny asks.

'That's what I'm here to find out.'

'I was into the Manchester music scene, you know *Mad*chester? Anyways, I met a girl, met her at a club here in DC playing all Manchester stuff and this girl, she was from Manchester. We started dating and she made me a Blue.'

I try my best to keep up with Jonny's quick patter; the man could win a rap battle without even knowing he's in one.

'I eventually moved here to DC from Virginia in 2005 and at first it was just me at Lucky Bar watching alone. I was the first one here. My friend Andrew was a Blue and he started joining me, but he left for San Francisco where he started his own supporters club. I stayed here and eventually met Tim, before that it was just a few friends I'd bribe to wear City shirts and hang out for the big matches at Lucky Bar.'

Jonny takes a proud scan of Lucky's back room and a swig from his Budweiser.

'I'll never forget the FA Cup semi-final in 2011, when I couldn't get anyone else to come. I was the only Blue, staring down 100 angry Reds. When we went up 1-0 I jumped up on the pool table and started shouting at them until my voice gave out. One of them finally yelled, "What ya gonna do, there's a hundred of us and only one of you?" I'd lost my voice and couldn't respond. This is when Lucky's Welsh bar owner Paul took to the stage, grabbed a microphone and informed the Reds over the PA system, "Jonny may be the only Blue here, but he drinks more than all of you put together, so you'll leave him be!"'

Jonny takes another haul from his beer, 'I used to party a lot back then, but I'm married now.

'Now look: it's 11am on a Sunday and we have 30 people out, all buying up membership cards. It's a testament to the Facebook page, it really is. Tim and I aren't great at organizing, but Matthew's Facebook work really made a huge difference. I'm not on Facebook, though.'

'Are you still in touch with the Mancunian girl?' I ask.

'You know, I probably haven't seen her in 12 years now.'

'What if you did see her again?' I ask.

'I guess if I ever did see her again, I would just like to say thank you.'

Jonny never mentions her name, and I know better than to ask.

During half-time, after a flaccid 45 minutes of scoreless footy, the supporters serenade Matthew with a chorus of Happy Birthday, and I get chatting with Walid Osmanzoi, who used to live in Germany and came to support city by way of a love for Bayern Munich, and utter disdain for Manchester United.

You may already have guessed the famous match that turned Walid Blue. On 26 May 1999, 12-year-old Walid was rendered heartbroken at the hands of a villainous club in red. Up 1-0 with only added time to play, it looked certain that Walid's treasured Bayern side were about to lift the Champions League trophy, the millennium's final kings of Europe. Then, shockingly, two goals in added time propelled Manchester United to the dreaded treble: FA Cup, Premier League, Champions League.

'I decided right then that, whoever United's rivals were, that was who I would follow in England. That's how I first got into City, but now, after 14 years I think I actually like City more than Bayern,' Walid confesses.

The two late goals are the sort of thing that almost never happens in football, yet, six days later, another championship match would play out in incredibly similar fashion. Manchester City, a full two leagues below the Premier Leagues, would pull off the most famous win in their history, storming back from 2-0 down with only five minutes of normal time remaining to draw level with Gillingham. A Nicky Weaver save in the penalties sent City back to the First Division and many supporters will tell you, 30 May 1999 was the day City's fortunes truly changed.

Lucky Bar is my first visit to a club that isn't strictly City and Walid tells me he prefers it this way; in fact many of the Blues here prefer things this way. In North America we're used to mixing supporters, we don't even separate them at live matches – not always a good idea in Philadelphia, mind you. There are no Cardiff City fans in the pub today, though I am told its Welsh owner very much wanted to be here. Apparently on City versus Arsenal matchdays the mood can grow fairly intense at Lucky Bar.

One post on DC's social media page that caught my eye leading up to this visit was from Anthony Youngblood. Anthony has a three-year-old son and the only way he was going to make the match was to bring him along after his soccer match earlier that morning. The Capital City Blues unanimously replied, 'Bring him along!'

Anthony arrives just in time for the second half, with son Anthony Youngblood the Second. This is his real name; I haven't made this up, and if he doesn't grow up to be an action hero, there is no justice in this world. A massive hit in his toddler-sized Argentina kit, AY2 (as Hollywood will one day market him) looks like a pint-sized Sergio Aguero.

Having young Timo and Anthony at the club adds a special element to the atmosphere and they will help us all remain calm and composed in language, as the coming 45 minutes of football are about to test our collective manners. In the months ahead two more posts from Anthony will catch my eye; the passing of his father and his relinquishing treasurer duties at Capital City Blues, as the US Navy officer ships out for active duty.

The second half starts with a cracking Edin Dzeko strike from well outside the box. It is City's fifth goal of the season without an answer from either opponent. If the season opener had me wondering if City would lose a match at all this year, today's performance has me questioning if they'll concede a single goal. I needn't wait long for an answer to both delusional fantasies. Seven minutes later, an Icelander from some tiny little place called Akureyri pounces on a rebound from a Cardiff shot that has left poor Joe Hart prostrate on the pitch. Aron Gunnarsson makes no mistake with his opportunity and belts home Cardiff City's first Premier League goal in 50 years. Cardiff City 1 Manchester City 1. Surely Cardiff won't score two.

If, on 25 August 2013, I had somehow placed a fiver on Cardiff City to storm back and win the match 3-2, Fraizer Campbell scoring two headers in the final 15 minutes, I could have financed the remainder of the journey with the winnings, staying in five-star hotels all along the way. But a team who hadn't been in the Premier League for 50 years beating the champions of 2012 was unimaginable – unless of course you follow City. On second thought, perhaps we all should have seen this coming.

A too-late strike from Negredo changes nothing. There will be no two-goal miracle comeback today.

In a season that was always going to be close, I find myself already worrying we've lost the league in week two, just six days after I was convinced we'd go unbeaten. Such is the roller coaster of irrational football thinking.

Washington, DC

We assemble for a while on the sidewalk, beside Lucky Bar, posing for pictures together and eating mouthwatering chorizo empanadas from Julia's next door. Moritz regretfully tells me he must leave as soon as matches are over as Timo suffers from a rare form of diabetes called diabetes insipidus. Timo, I am thrilled to report, is doing great as of our last check-in, but on this day, dad and son head off for a well-deserved rest.

I finally learn that 'DC Cap's' real name is Adam Rausch and that once, in Wales, he and a mate found a pub serving chicken wings so cheap they ate six dozen. Jonny sticks around for a while and tells me I absolutely must get up to New York City and see the gang at The

Mad Hatter. Off to the side, Matthew confers with his girlfriend Liz about taking me to view the new City In The Community pitches being built at Marie Reed Elementary School in the Adams Morgan neighbourhood of DC. From what I can hear, it's a bit of a journey from Lucky Bar, so I interrupt the decision-making and assure them I'll be just fine discovering the magic of DC on my own today. I've mapped out a few things I'd like to see: Ford's Theatre where Lincoln was shot, the giant paintings on the walls of the Renwick Gallery and Bobby's Burger Palace on K Street, near the corner of 18th. None will disappoint.

Outside Lucky Bar, empanadas consumed, match over, the Capital City Blues decide it is time to say our goodbyes. But not before a stirring rendition of a song Chris Nield once taught me in a crowded pub in Manchester's Northern Quarter.

> *We never win at home and we never win away*
> *We lost last week and we lost today*
> *We don't give a fuck, 'cos we're all pissed up*
> *MCFC OK*

That's 364 miles down, 43,418 to go.

3
NEW YORK CITY

Grand Forks

INITIALLY I had scheduled New York for the following week's derby, but again, life has a funny way of poking its nose in and changing things. As I sat in Opera Bob's one late-July evening brainstorming this book idea with a few of the lads and trying to think of ways to raise money for the journey, JC Plante – Opera Bob's 2012 Man of the Year – tapped me on the shoulder and quietly asked,

'When were you planning on New York?'

'Derby day, September 22,' I replied.

JC whispered back, 'If you go on the 14th, I'll come with you and pay for your flight and hotel.'

So here I am eight weeks later in the departures lounge at Toronto's Island Airport having a bit of fun with JC at the expense of a mad businesswoman with a curiously outdated laptop, a knapsack instead of briefcase and a business vernacular JC assures me no one has used in ten years.

It's Friday 13 September, just before noon in the middle of a quiet airport lounge. The woman in question has her fingertips in the powerful pyramid formation and, with a set of earbuds jammed in her ears, shouts out shit like, 'Benchmarks! Timelines! Goals!'

'I doubt there's even anyone on the other end of this call,' I joke with JC, before getting up to grab us another round of Rolling Rock beer and iced tea. We laugh in agreement and get ready to fly to New York City.

An easy 90-minute flight later, we land in Newark, a couple of bums from Hogtown (a centuries-old slight against Toronto) ready for a weekend in the Big Apple, a much cooler nickname, with ties to horse racing in the 1920s. After waiting in a customs line longer than our flight down, we're on a train bound for one of the most exciting cities on the planet. I've been to New York many times before; it never gets old and you could live three lifetimes here and never come close to experiencing all it has to offer.

Do *not* live your life without at least one visit to New York City.

Of all the great things about New York, its pizza may be the greatest. By the time JC and I finally arrive in Manhattan we're starving, and our first slice doesn't disappoint. In fact the slices at Giuseppe's on Lexington, between 39th and 40th, are so good we decide to order another full pizza just to have in our hotel room at all times.

This decision will prove equal parts genius and disgusting over the course of our weekend.

JC has splashed out on an absolute cracker of a Manhattan hotel and it's a far cry from my last time in New York, which was spent in Brooklyn, sharing a closet-sized room for two with three bandmates.

By sheer coincidence I have a few friends in town this weekend, and the first plan was for everyone to meet on the rooftop bar of the hotel for drinks then head back to the room for a peaceful sleep, assuring we'll be sharp for City's 10am kick-off versus Stoke. Fortunately JC yanked my head out from my ass and my boring plan has changed to meeting our friends in Little Italy.

The 87th annual Feast of San Gennaro is in full swing by the time JC and I get to Lower Manhattan. The streets are packed full of mobile food trucks, restaurants with teeming patios and herds of people from Long Island. Rows of tiny white lights sway between the buildings forming an uneven archway that we stroll under for a few blocks, until arriving at Da Nico Ristorante. On the surface, Da Nico appears to be a tiny restaurant, but after being led to its giant back terrace, I feel like we've discovered a hidden gem. Walking past their wall of fame however, I accept that this eatery is no secret; the people who have eaten here range from New York Yankee superstars all the way up to President Clinton.

We score a table in the very back corner of the garden and settle in for the first of many bottles of wine. To my immediate left, sitting at the head of our table is Alex Nassar, one of my oldest friends from childhood, and the guy who insists he once saw a man vacuuming his front lawn. Beside Alex sits his girlfriend Hillary, the two in town to visit Alex's mother who lives in the Bronx. Beside Hillary is Kim Gardner. Kim lives and works in New York now, but spent ten years in Toronto, nine of which were spent dating my best mate. To Kim's right at the opposite head of the table is our man JC, looking as Canadian as ever with his flowing dark hair and a bushy beard that has my patchy Spanish-euro-beard feeling rather envious. Directly to my right is where things get a little more complicated. My ex-girlfriend from Barcelona just happened to choose the same weekend to visit Kim. So here we are: childhood friend, hard-drinking Blue, best mate's ex, and my ex.

Drinks please.

Alex, perhaps sensing the initial awkwardness, swiftly orders a round of six limoncellos. I'm not one for the sweet lemon-based Italian liqueur. Nor is Hillary or Kim, for that matter. JC, never one to let a proper drink go to waste, assembles the five discarded flutes and downs them in quick succession. This display gets everyone in the spirit, many bottles of red wine and Peroni follow and I get to catch up with some of my dearest friends, all due to the generosity of one of my newer consorts. JC and I stagger back to our hotel room around 3am, not too shabby for night one in New York City.

Morning arrives too soon (especially for the one who necked five limoncellos) but New York holds such promise of excitement that hangovers don't seem to last as long here. A quick shower followed by half a slice of day-old pizza and we're both good as new. Out the door by 9.45am sharp for the short cab ride over to experience New York's official Manchester City supporters club.

Saturday 14 September. Stoke City v City. 10am kick-off

A nearly indescribable pride comes from witnessing your club's presence in the heart of the world's most famous city. Arriving at the corner of 3rd Street and East 26th to find The Mad Hatter, Boddingtons sign in the front window and a large City flag draped across the entrance, is enough to place a proud lump in even the most hardened supporter's throat.

The inside of The Mad Hatter is jaw-dropping. The bar sits to your immediate right and it doesn't just lead your eye, it dominates with its gorgeous wooden awning, smooth curves, and expert craftsmanship. It looks like this bar has been here since the early days of New York City itself.

The wall behind the bar features three giant mirrors, each bearing a giant gold-leaf logo in its centre: The Mad Hatter's logo in the middle, to the left the three lions of England and to the far right, nearest the entrance, is the classiest City emblem I've ever laid eyes on.

Kevin Jones is the man credited for starting the Hatter Blues, but unfortunately, he can't be here today. Again: it's Stoke, it's Sunday, it's September and this is all completely understandable. My contact for today will be Daryl 'Grandsolo' Brown, a man who, if you come to New York, you do not want to miss meeting. Daryl was born in Manchester, and at the age of seven moved to the Bronx, his infectious accent entirely the latter. Daryl's frame is more in line with an American footballer than an English one, and I'm starting to think he and Moritz would form an intimidating offensive line.

Daryl shows me around the pub with great pride and informs me they've just renovated during the summer. From their back patio with a giant screen to the bevelled copper in the new tables, surrounded by City paraphernalia, Heart of the City award, old matchday programmes framed and placed lovingly on the wall, and to top it off, an old red telephone booth turned into a wine rack, front to back The Mad Hatter is exquisite.

JC and I find a table near one of the Hatter's three glorious HD TVs and order up a round of double-egg, chips and beans from the Hatter's British-dominated brunch menu.

The long-anticipated Stoke City versus Manchester City mid-September clash finally kicks off and I can't recall a more boring half of football in my life.

I have nothing more to say on it, other than it was painful to witness.

The regal taps at The Mad Hatter stand at the ready, like the Queen's Guard. Four authentic hand-pumped ale taps, which include the obligatory London Pride and Bombardier, another dozen or so taps for lager and one special tap, near to my heart, pouring liquid gold – Boddingtons Pub Ale. I usually prefer to drink local beers on my travels, but I can't resist the Boddingtons on tap; not always easy to find in North America, this morning it is a must.

During the half-time break Daryl Grandsolo – a moniker he earned DJ'ing New York City clubs – gets on the mic and hosts a 50/50 draw with proceeds benefitting their local City In The Community initiative. Following the raffle he pops by our table with wife Stephanie and recalls their one-year anniversary spent in Niagara Falls – and Opera Bob's.

'I said we'd go to Niagara Falls, so long as we could watch the FA Cup semi-final match against United. So we decided to drive up to Toronto and watch the match there,' Daryl says.

'Have you tried that pulled pork sandwich at Opera Bob's?' Stephanie jumps in.

'I haven't actually,' I reply.

'That was the best pulled pork sandwich I've had. I want to visit again just for that!' she replies.

I can't help but feel a tinge of hometown pride hearing a native New Yorker compliment Toronto cuisine and I'm excited at the thought of telling our cook 'Hoss' the good news that word of his sandwich is spreading.

Stephanie has adopted City by association and while she loves the boys in blue, is still a bit perplexed by Daryl's intensity for his hometown club.

'He shouts at the referees you know,' she tells me before turning her attention to him, 'like they can hear you?'

'I think we're all guilty of that from time to time,' I confess.

'He shouts at the referees on his PlayStation!'

'But, that's a computer; I'm not sure they can get a call wrong.'

'I keep telling him that!' Stephanie insists.

Daryl laments the turnout for today, around 25 or so, is not indicative of a derby or major showdown at The Mad Hatter, and I remind him this is the case at any supporters club with an early September morning kick-off.

'What was this place like on *the day*?' I ask.

Daryl's eyes instantly travel back to one of the best days in any Blue's life; 13 May 2012. Earlier, when I stated that 30 May 1999 versus Gillingham was City's most famous comeback, there may have been some of you protesting such an assertion. And if you were, you likely hold the day we won our first league title in 44 years as City's most magical feat. And you have a strong case.

On the morning of 13 May 2012, Manchester City looked certain to lift their first championship trophy in my lifetime. By mid-afternoon these hopes had all but disappeared – and what's worse, the trophy was headed to our rivals.

Needing a win over 17th-placed Queens Park Rangers, with only five minutes of added time to play, City found themselves up a man yet incredibly, down a goal. I remember sitting in the third tier of the Etihad with my brother-in-law, promising myself I would never again watch, not just a City match, but any sporting event again.

No more Toronto Maple Leafs, no baseball, no boxing, nothing. Sport, I decided, is simply too cruel.

Then, a header from Edin Dzeko levelled the score. But surely it was too late. Half of the stadium began to cheer on our Blues, while the other half remained convinced there wasn't enough time left and that City drawing level actually served to make the experience even more painful.

In the final minute of added time, Sergio Aguero, a man who will never pay for another beer, or dinner, or likely even a car, in Manchester ever again, darted through the entire QPR squad and cemented City's place in football history. The most incredible conclusion to a season any of us are likely ever to see.

'You see this floor here?' an animated Daryl asks, pointing to the hardwood planks beneath his feet. 'I swore it was gonna buckle!'

Perhaps sensing my disbelief that a street-level floor could somehow buckle, Daryl pulls out his phone – the screen is smashed to bits – and through the splintered shards I watch an incredible video.

Daryl wasn't lying about the size of the crowd that day; it's easily pushing the Hatter's 300-person capacity. With the camera shaking and Blues going mental, it's hard to make anything else out, save for one thing: a familiar figure front and centre, jumping higher and screaming louder than any other Blue in the moshpit of revelling Citizens. Through the shaking camera work and broken screen I make out an unmistakable figure, wearing a large pair of blue aviator-style sunglasses.

'Hey, is that guy's name…'

'Yeah, that's Jonny Danish alright,' Daryl says.

The second half is more of the same from City and their Midland rivals, and unless you had £1,000 on the 0-0 draw, you wouldn't recall much of what will likely be the dullest match of the year. It occurs to me that City are actually off to what now seems a bit of a shaky start. Two home wins, but only one of a possible six points on the road has me wondering if perhaps this season under our new Chilean manager might be one designated with that terrifying word 'transition'.

After the most impotent match of football you could ever imagine, I sit down with Kyron Rogers, or 'Kai' as he's more affectionately called among the New York City Blues. Kai chose City as they seemed the appropriate footballing parallel to his beloved New York Mets baseball club, an association many New Yorkers identify with. The Mets wear a lighter shade of blue than their rivals in the Bronx and have 25 fewer championship titles to their name than the world-famous Yankees, which causes me to wonder if perhaps City should have twinned with the Mets instead of the Yankees.

I have a brief chat with John Pepper, who teaches economics in Connecticut and most weekends drives nearly three hours each way to watch City at The Hatter. Pep is in charge of memberships and sheds interesting light on to the split of expats to New Yorkers at The Mad Hatter.

'I've sold 45 member cards already this season and at least 30 of them were to Americans. The club keeps changing, it's evolving.'

By the end of this season the official paid membership will be nearly 100, not to mention the hundreds more who will visit as travelling Blues. Two excellent examples of visiting Blues are Melanie and Greg, here from Manchester on holiday. When I ask them how they found The Mad Hatter, Melanie looks at me as though I've lived under a rock my entire life. 'It's famous!' she replies.

With much love and respect to all the Blues I'll meet this weekend, no one could be more entertaining than The

Mad Hatter's co-owner and Liverpool supporter Michael Traynor. JC and I are just about to make our way back to the hotel when the smiling, salt-and-pepper-haired Michael pulls up a seat at our table and in the world's greatest accent ask us, 'Right lads, what's all this you're up to then?'

After briefly explaining the book idea to Michael, JC and I are privileged to spend the next hour and a half hanging on his every story. The life-long Liverpool supporter owns one of the most impressive Manchester City supporter pubs you will ever find. Over complimentary pints of Boddingtons he tells JC and I about how he came to New York in the 1980s determined not to enter the bar industry. But as Michael puts it, 'There were only two jobs for the Irish in 1980s New York: construction or bartending. And after two weeks of construction I decided it was too cold and my hands were far too delicate for construction.'

My favourite story of Michael's – and there are many – involves an innocent lie and a gorgeous woman.

'I got so tired of answering the "Where is your accent from?" question that I decided to choose the most remote spot I could find on the American map and make that my new answer.'

Michael dangles his index finger over our table.

'I held my finger over the map and found the place, smack! Grand Forks, North Dakota. Perfect, no one will have heard of that.'

'Had you ever been to Grand Forks?' I ask.

'Never, not to this day. But for years I got away with telling customers at the bar I was the proud product of Grand Forks, North Dakota.'

'Did that work?' JC asks.

'It worked for years, until one evening, when the most gorgeous woman I'd ever seen in my life walked in and sat at the bar. After a while of chatting, she asked me where I was from and it was just a reflex by this point. "Grand Forks North Dakota," I said. "You're kidding me!" she shouts, "That's where I'm from!" Then she asks me, "Which part of Grand Forks are you from?'"

'How'd you answer that?' I ask excitedly.

'Simple. Main Street.'

JC bursts into his signature high-pitched laugh, which is in absolute contrast to his burly lumberjack appearance. I pat Michael on the shoulder and order us up another round.

I think my lasting image of The Mad Hatter will forever be that of Michael Traynor poking his head through the front window of his pub and shouting 'cheers lads' in his charming Irish timbre, as JC and I climb into a taxi bound for a hotel room filled with leftover slices of the best pizza in the world.

4
CHICAGO

You Lucky Bastard

THERE IS a notorious song, sung by a small minority of City supporters, involving former Manchester United manager Alex Ferguson and a bouncy castle. The song is not my favourite, a bit too harsh for my genial nature. When it comes to giving Sir Alex a bit of banter, I prefer such Fergie-related hits as 'You Signed Phil Jones', 'Fergie, Fergie Sign 'im Up' or my all-time favourite, 'You Lucky Bastards, it Should Have Been Ten', referencing the time we beat our fiercest rivals 6-1 at their own ground. Still, it is hard to see a bouncy castle and not think of our famous enemy.

Victoria Gregory grew up in Sheffield, the younger daughter of Mancunian parents Etta and David Gregory. David was away a lot with the Royal Navy, but instilled in his daughter a deep love for the boys from Maine Road. Victoria is one of the founding members of the official supporters club in Chicago, a job opportunity having brought her here five years ago, and as we are both contributing bloggers on the Manchester City website, we were in touch before this trip began. In one exchange Victoria mentioned a few friends were going to the Jake Bugg concert the night before the derby and she asked if I would like to join them.

So I fly into Chicago a day early, throw on my Man City Originals jumper – a particularly nice one this season with leather patches on the elbows and understated badge of leather identifying MCFC – and meet Victoria and her friends for pre-show drinks where the famous pool scenes from *The Color Of Money* were shot: the Gingerman Tavern in the Wrigleyville neighbourhood of Chicago.

On the cab ride over, I receive a text from Victoria, which reads, 'I'm standing by the jukebox and I'm a bit drunk.'

Once I arrive, I quickly find Victoria, indeed by the jukebox and definitely a little tipsy. She is joined by four of her friends, all of whom are English, none of whom are Blue. Mark, a Notts County supporter, is aware of what has brought me to his adopted country, and after our first pint he tells me, 'Put this in your book.'

Mark's story isn't a Manchester City story, it's a Notts County one. But I can appreciate the parallels between the two clubs as City were in many ways Notts County not all that long ago: away matches to grounds resembling cow pastures, multi-goal losses to towns with impossible-to-pronounce names and players who moonlighted as postmen and rubbish collectors.

'I flew back for the Nottingham derby when we drew Forest in the League Cup, two seasons ago. All 30 of my cousin's mates were Forest and I had to sit in the home section with them. With County up 2-1 late in the match, my cousin shouted, "Mate, I can't bear to watch you beat us!" and promptly got up and left the ground. On the last kick of regular time, Wes Morgan shinned one in for Forest to go to penalties. We lost 3-2 in the end but my cousin wasn't there to witness it, so as far as I'm concerned, we won the match 2-1.'

After a good few drinks at the Gingerman, we head next door to The Metro for the Jake Bugg concert 'feeling no pain', as my dad would say.

This is the sort of outing I avoid at all costs these days. I've moved on from music and found what I think is a promising alternative in writing, but it still won't be easy watching a 19-year-old with his whole life ahead of him grace the stage in a world full of everything I so desperately wanted. I remember turning 21 in Australia, having just appeared on a television show alongside Green Day and believing – naively, as 21-year-old men often do – that this is just the way life was meant to unfold. I tried for ten more years to get back to that level and never did, plying my trade instead in that cruel artistic purgatory between outrageous success and unsustainable poverty.

Once inside The Metro, we meet an angry Chelsea supporter, who was apparently denied an autograph for he and his missus, and this has completely set him off.

'There are only two things I hate in this world: Manchester United and Jake fucking Bugg!' he shouts. The 40-something Englishman, with an accent from somewhere in London – hell if I can ever pin those down – wears his girlfriend's black bra strapped around his head, reminiscent of Wayne Rooney's protective head gear.

The Brits I'm with all laugh and chant 'Rooney, Rooney' as the good-natured Chelsea supporter bounces around to the opening act. As I will come to learn more and more along this journey, not all Chelsea supporters are your stereotypical football hooligans; we share a good laugh and a few pints with the jilted Bugg fan.

The Metro Concert Hall fits Chicago's art-deco aesthetic completely, a gorgeous venue with a small balcony and opera-house-style stage. With the opening act still performing, The Metro's 1,150 capacity appears already reached. I am at the bar, holding court with Victoria and her friend Nicky, who is visiting from London.

So far the evening is flawless (minus Nicky being a Red). This gang are exactly my kind of people, full-speed-ahead fun and it's still 12 hours to go until the derby kicks off. The good feeling changes, or at least is interrupted, when Jake Bugg finally hits the stage. I am quickly reminded there is nothing on Earth – save for maybe a fireman carrying a baby from a burning building – that can compete for a person's attention quite like a singer on his or her stage.

'Come on, we're going to the front of the stage!' shouts Victoria, pulling my hand and trying to get me to follow her and Nicky. I tell them I'll find them, 'Just need to hit the loo first,' as though using British vernacular somehow makes it okay.

With no intention of following, I retreat to the back bar and order myself another beer. All of my insecurities and regret have come rushing back. I remember being the object of a crowd's attention, hundreds to Jake's thousands mind you, but still, I know what it feels like to have fans at the front of the stage, singing along to something I wrote. I shouldn't be in Chicago writing a City book, I should be here at The Metro, singing.

Another pint later I find myself alone in the toilets for a piss, the rest of the world out front doing exactly what they came here to do, enjoy an up-and-coming musician at the top of his game. Am I really going to feel sorry for myself in Chicago on a Friday night? I zip up and have a very serious conversation with myself in he mirror, 'You *are* here to write! Music is over and you are here for the story. Life is good. Really good. Stop taking yourself so seriously, get the hell out there and for the first time in your 36 years, push yourself through a screaming crowd, get to the front of that god-damned stage and join your new friends!'

I manage to wade through about five rows of what must easily be 30, when my plan takes an interesting and dangerous turn. I feel someone grab at my elbow. I turn to discover a stunning blonde woman in a pink dress, slim black belt and piercing blue eyes, which would melt the heart of even the hardest West Ham supporter.

'I like your sweater,' she shouts above the jangling guitars.

'It's Manchester City,' I tell her, not knowing what else to say.

She's never heard of them and asks what brings me to Chicago. I briefly tell her about the book; she seems interested and I can't help but feel like I'm entering a world of trouble here.

'I'm Natasha,' she tells me. And I wonder why all beautiful women seem to bear names that perfectly match their looks.

We spend the rest of the concert shouting above the music and ruining the show for some poor guy behind us, whom I think likely had his eye on Natasha before I stumbled along.

When the final encore is over, Natasha asks me to join her and her friends at their next stop, and there are two reasons why I must decline. One, I am an invited guest of Victoria and her friends, they've been absolutely brilliant, and tonight I will go where they go. The second reason is, of course, Jess.

Natasha tells me she'd love to read the book when it's done and so of course, we must exchange phone numbers.

We even discuss the possibility of a dinner later in my visit. As we part ways I hope very sincerely to never see Natasha again, but I know it won't be long before I do.

The rest of the night is spent bar-hopping, ingesting famous Weiner Circle hot dogs – the highlight of which is a staff who absolutely berate you while you wait for your food, a true Chicago *must* – and finally Victoria and I serenading the locals from our moving taxi, 'It should have been ten, you lucky bastards, it should have been ten!'

I awake in a lonely hotel room in downtown Chicago, to one of the top-ten hangovers of my life. It isn't necessarily that I drank *more* than I ever have, rather, in my mid-30s even a few draught beers are starting to hurt the next day. And we certainly imbibed more than a few pints of draught beer. It's 8.30am and the first Manchester derby of the season kicks off in 90 minutes. Time to get to work. Ouch.

There's no time for the L Train. I'm going to have to shower up, sober up and jump in another cab. The previous night I enjoyed a cab ride more than worth its fare. The driver was a Chelsea supporter from Sierra Leone, and we talked footy the full 20-minute ride to the pub and I easily could have enjoyed another 20, he being intensely knowledgeable about footy and endlessly interesting in a story that took him from Sierra Leone, to London, and finally here to Chicago. Hell, we even talked about ice hockey.

This morning's cabbie is similar in terms of his geniality, and appears up for a chat. I feel bad that I can't offer back more than a few forced and painful groans. This is the exact moment I decide the rest of this adventure *must* be done sober and I tell myself that as wretched as this hangover feels, at least I can take consolation in the knowledge that it will be my last.

As we pass the imposing shores of Lake Michigan I'm enveloped in all kinds of cruel hung-over introspection. I want to tell the cabbie to pull over. I want to get out and wade into the second largest of the Great Lakes, allowing its crashing waves to peel the guilt off me, even though I don't really have anything to feel poorly about, other than an innocent late-night text between me and Natasha.

I rest my head against the cold taxi window, which offers a small amount of relief as I watch morning joggers stride confidently down the Lakeshore Path, outfitted in high-end running gear worth more than my best suit. The fibres on these models of health hug their alcohol-free-lifestyle curves and do nothing to help me feel any better about myself. I fucking hate joggers.

Sunday 22 September. City v United. 10am kick-off

I step into the Globe Pub, 1934 West Irving Park Road, Chicago, Illinois, at 9.30am. If the fittingly globe-shaped sign out front looks familiar, it should; turns out I got drunk here last night. Inside, a narrow front room, the identical adjacent room and smaller back room look familiar, and last night begins to come back to me.

'Oh my God I did shots,' I realize as another blood vessel bursts somewhere behind my right eye. What doesn't look familiar, nor is it comforting, is the sea of *red* rippling through the bar. For a worrisome 30 seconds I am too hung-over to realize it's merely Arsenal red. The Globe is a mixed-supporter pub and the Gooners are playing the early match today, phew! The few United fans who are in attendance desperately paw at their cellphones trying to figure out where Chicago's United pub might be located.

I rediscover the Blue section of the Globe exactly where it was the night before, at the end of room one, underneath the shrine to Manchester City that includes a framed picture of Mike Summerbee in his playing days, another of Buzzer during his visit with the Chicago Blues and, most importantly, the Globe's official Heart Of The City award.

The first two people I see this morning are the final two I saw last night; Victoria and Nicky look exactly the way I feel. The two who were so full of life just a few short hours ago, best friends divided by red and blue, are this morning the very same shade of pale green. Rivalries aside, we're all in this hangover together.

The first glimmer of hope that today's hangover might go differently than those in my miserable post-drunk past is the arrival of Mark Zanatta. Mark – a man who once famously donated ten dollars to the Opera Bob's C-word jar in a single day – is originally from St Catharines, Ontario, a short 90-minute drive south from where I grew up. Mark is my age and we quickly fall into the familiar obscure-reference-based patter shared only between those born in the same year and region of the world.

A rowing scholarship brought Mark to the States, a job kept him here a while longer, and children eventually deemed that Chicago would be home. When I quietly confide my hangover status to Mark, he instructs me to, 'Get back on the horse. It's the only way.'

I let Mark know there is zero chance my body could consume alcohol today without projectile consequences. Nevertheless, Mark's mere arrival has brought my hangover down from a nine out of ten to a slightly more survivable eight.

A nervous energy circulates around The Globe as our City heroes appear in the tunnel, some 3,800 miles away at the Etihad. Victoria proudly points out to me where on the tunnel wall her name resides. If I'm to be totally honest, I don't enjoy derbies. Many supporters live for them, but my stomach is the sort that twists into painful coils when Red lines up against Blue. If I could be guaranteed a win, I'd watch with a large crowd every time, but the level of uncertainty both in relation to the scoreline and my propensity to throw things should the day not go our way, means I'd be more comfortable watching this match alone in some cabin deep in the Canadian wilderness.

Here in a packed-out Chicago pub I am a nervous wreck and City's shaky form of late is not helping matters. The Chicago MCFC scarf I've just been given – the sharpest scarf of all the supporters clubs in my opinion – is already wound tightly around my cheeks and nearly over my eyes. I hate derby day until I love it, that's how it goes.

The match kicks off and the Arsenal supporters, along with one Chelsea-kitted gentleman, come over to join the Blue side of The Globe, easily 40 strong by now, and with the pub's narrow dimensions we're all shoulder-to-shoulder, precisely the way football should be enjoyed. The first Manchester derby of the season is underway and it won't be long before a party is, too.

City look good to start, really good in fact, and it makes me even more nervous. I convince myself they look *too* good if that is somehow possible. I'm certain we will dominate the game only to lose to a fluky last-minute Fergie-time goal. Only this season there is no Fergie and things are already feeling a bit different.

One of the Gooners, his team having just done away with Stoke 3-1, appears ready to start trouble at any moment. Shaved head, long goatee and sleeve tattoos on both arms. He's American for sure, a biker perhaps, and not to be messed with beyond a doubt. Better keep my eye on him. Fortunately I'm standing beside Mark who is easily the biggest and – as so often is the case with big dudes – friendliest guy in the pub.

Enough people seem to know this *Sons of Anarchy*-looking character they're calling Gary and none seem worried the banter will escalate into anything more serious. I'll trust the locals' read on the situation, but still keep my place next to my big Canadian brother in case shit does go down.

In the 16th minute I mercifully slide down another rung on the hangover ladder, from eight to seven, when Aleksandar Kolarov whips a sublime cross into Aguero and Sergio swings his left leg – into a position mine couldn't achieve were two bodybuilders to try and yank it there – and smashes the ball into the back of the net.

The Globe explodes in a manner and volume no place on this journey has to date. As I feel the floor shake and watch the Poznan get underway I can't help but feel this is the moment I've waited for. All the self-doubt, self-loathing and uncertainty regarding this project exits in one glorious wonder strike from Sergio Kun Aguero; his 50th as a Blue.

It doesn't take long for my derby day anxiety to return and the scarf is once again tightly pulled around my cheekbones. I begin to consider the likelihood we'll blow this early lead. I turn to Victoria and tell her, 'I really think we need another, I'd feel much more comfortable two up.'

Just before half-time, Yaya Touré, my mother's favourite Ivorian, knocks a corner in off his knee. A ball that might have found its way wide a few years ago under Alex Ferguson's sorcery instead dribbles past a baffled David de Gea and comes to rest on the more meaningful side of United's goal line. City are up 2-0 going into the break and the temptation to get back on the horse is growing stronger by the minute.

I must admit to feeling slightly badly for Victoria's Red mate Nicky and I respect what a true friend she is to Victoria, for it is true friendship to accompany your mate to an official Blue bar as a Red and sit there desperately hungover and endure your team getting absolutely torn apart by its biggest rival.

Vic and Nicky met bartending in Greece 15 years ago and have been best mates ever since. Despite only knowing them for less than 24 hours I am already convinced their days in Greece would make a scandalous book of its own, perhaps my third, after *Jonny Danish: the Party Years*. I tell Nicky I'm impressed she has come, and she confides in me that she doesn't see a way back for United. 'I reckon City will get two more,' she says.

A job at Ladbrokes just may be in her future.

It's half-time in Chicago, The Globe is absolutely buzzing and Mark Zanatta is trying his hardest to get me drinking again. It brings me back to the time in Manchester when Chris Nield and his dad, Ian, brought me to the Waldorf to watch an early away kick-off versus Liverpool. I was also hungover on that day, and Chris taught me that Heineken was a solid hangover pint. The logic sounded counterintuitive to me, but a few hours later as I swayed hopelessly through the Arndale in search of fish and chips, I can tell you this much: I was no longer hung-over.

During a brief alcohol-bullying break Mark describes Chicago's municipal flag hanging on the wall behind us and how well suited it is to City. Sky-blue bars on white, with four stars in the centre. One hopes it is not only colour appropriate but prophetic in some way. Next, Mark moves back to the booze talk and tells me of a local Chicago shot known as a 'Malört'. He admits to having no clue what is actually in Malört, just that, 'There may be some wormwood involved and the taste won't leave your mouth for a full 24 hours.'

'Jesus, what is a hangover on Malört like?' I ask.

'You don't drink multiple shots of Malört. If you get drunk on Malört, you die,' he says.

I manage to avoid the pressure of half-time drinks, but two minutes into the second half Sergio puts us up three goals to the good and even the most cynical City fan now knows that for today at least, the city is ours! Down two more rungs on the hangover ladder, it is only a matter of time before I'm back on that horse.

Three minutes later, it's 4-0 thanks to Jesus's pace along the wing, his graceful cross in and Vinny Kompany making things extra-tricky by joining the rush. It's an easy blast home from Nasri, whose celebration would become the most iconic image of the now famous day. I drop my scarf from around my mouth, down to its proper resting place and proudly proclaim to my new Chicago family, 'If City win 6-0 I'm doing a shot of Malört!' I quickly see that Chicagoans take such decries quite seriously and I have never hoped more in my life for a final scoreline of 5-0.

Thankfully for my Malört-fearing liver, that's all the scoring required from City. The full-time whistle blows on a historic 4-1 victory. Monica, our bartender, pours 35 flutes of champagne to celebrate and it's time to get back on that horse. Perhaps a nice hangover-Heineken I'm thinking? My first drink, however, will not be beer, and it arrives courtesy of an unexpected donor.

Gary Winters, aka the intimidating biker-looking Gooner I worried might start trouble at any moment, waltzes behind the bar as though he owns the place, extends his right hand and thanks me for coming; wouldn't you know it, Gary does co-own the place. And he's a brilliant character. He re-introduces Monica, whom I've already met, and puts down three empty shot glasses in front of us. It is Sunday at 12.05pm.

'What are we having?' Gary demands.

'Gary, I'm still way too rough from last night for shots.' I am adamant in my response.

Surely a fast-living man such as Gary will respect that I had an epic night of drinking in Chicago last night, and appreciate that much of it was done in his pub.

'That's not what I asked,' he replies. Gary glares daggers, first at the empty shot glasses, then deep into my eyes. If both hands and one foot were tied behind his back, Gary could still kick my ass.

'Either you choose a shot, or I'll choose it for you.'

I quickly determine there is no way out of this one. Time to harness my inner Waldorf.

'Okay Gary, you choose, but *not* whisky, whisky gets me into trouble,' I confess.

And I'm not at all lying. If there is one drink I must avoid at all costs, it's the alluring warmth of fermented grain mash and its ability to convince me I am 6ft 4in, 220lb and completely indestructible.

Gary returns with a bottle I've never seen before, and places it calmly before us, 'This is 70-proof and tastes like Jäger, only better,' he insists.

The drink is called Kabanes and the label features an old man resembling your standard Greek accordion player. Monica carefully pours three shots; we all down them in one and slam the empty glasses on the bar. The locals appear satisfied – for now.

The Globe has 44 paid members, up 83 per cent from the previous season, and the majority are American, an encouraging trend I'm noticing. The three original members at The Globe are Warren Garlick, Andrew

Tripp, and Matt Darst – Matt being the member Warren and Andrew credit with really getting things moving and organized. Matt, for the record, is extremely humble, thankful, and not at all convinced he deserves the credit. The lads assure me later that he absolutely does.

Warren Garlick fell in love with an American woman and moved to Chicago from Oldham only three years ago. Over his shoulder stands Nigel, a few years older than Warren. Nigel tells me that in 1992 he moved from Manchester for an American woman, eventually marrying his boss. Today is Nigel's first time at The Globe; make that 45 members.

Andrew Tripp is Brooklyn-born-and-raised, and at only 22 he is the youngest of the Chicago Blues. Andrew rivals Mark in height and like myself is attempting a beard that could use a little help.

As I sit back and listen, now comfortably enjoying a post-Kabanes pint of local craft beer, a warm buzz already reaching my toes, I notice one member in the corner wearing last year's purple goalie shirt. There's always one lad – *never* two – at these pubs wearing the keeper's shirt, and he is *always* worth speaking with. I wave him over for a chat and he introduces himself as Paul and his girlfriend, Mariateresa, whom the Chicago Blues affectionately call 'Mother'. Mother is so tiny the Chicago Blues often celebrate a win by throwing her high above their heads.

We now have the gang who will occupy our next three hours. There will be guest appearances, but the pints and stories, which are about to flow, will be told mostly between a semicircle of Mark, Warren, Matt, Andrew, Paul, Mother, and myself.

Victoria would have no doubt been right in there with us had she not been such a loyal friend to Nicky and realized that sticking around after a 4-1 defeat is likely too great an ask of someone with a hung-over night-flight back to England. We say our goodbyes and I promise to look Nicky up if I make it to London; she's one of the good Reds. As for Victoria, this weekend will prove to be the beginning of a long friendship.

The gang has set up shop on prime Chicago real estate, 30 paces inside The Globe Pub, directly in front of the main bar. The stories and pints that follow are expertly told and flawlessly poured. This is my version of heaven. Paul tells us about the time he scoped out Liam Gallagher's hotel bar only to end up drinking with the iconic singer from Burnage and his Beady Eye crew. You often hear negative stories regarding Liam Gallagher, but Paul's story is completely refreshing and a few other similar tales I will be told along the way will show Liam in an entirely new light for me.

'Liam sat down and said "alright", Paul explains. 'Then I said "alright". Then we talked about City, and his upcoming Beady Eye show. Nearly an hour later, as we got up to leave, Liam stuck his hand out to me and my mate Umaar and said, "Alright Paul, alright Umaar, good to meet you." As soon as he left, we went outside and danced around in the street like little girls at the fact Liam Gallagher remembered our names!'

The gang quickly informs me that Liam isn't the only target of Paul's Manchester music affection and that his nickname around The Globe is in fact 'The Stalker'. And who is the stalked? None other than fellow Blue himself, Johnny Marr. This leads Matt and Paul into a telling story about the time Morrissey came to The Globe that explains the difference in their minds between a Red and a Blue.

'I mean the whole story comes down to this: why come here if you don't want to be bothered? Why come to the one pub in Chicago where everyone is going to know exactly who you are and immediately post to Twitter the fact you're here?' Matt begins.

'So Morrissey, after another one of his infamous cancelled shows, strolled into The Globe a few years back and had them section off the back room. Absolutely no one outside of his entourage was allowed in there. I just wandered over to use the cash machine, having no idea anyone was there. I pulled back the curtain and holy shit, there's Morrissey! He stays for nearly two hours, refusing all pictures and autographs, I'm told, and then leaves the pub dramatically with his coat pulled over his head.'

'Mariateresa and I were out for dinner in Vegas and there's Johnny Marr and his wife sitting a few tables away!' Paul says, taking over.

'Don't be fooled; it was no coincidence Paul chose that restaurant,' Matt says.

'Okay, Mariateresa and I *do* follow Johnny around a *little* bit. But anyways, Johnny puts down what he's doing and sets aside at least ten minutes to talk with Mariateresa and me. And that's the difference between Morrissey and Johnny Marr, you see. The difference between Red and Blue,' Paul concludes.

Around this time a very bubbly and extremely cute blonde girl in a brand-new Vincent Kompany kit pops by and introduces herself. Her name is Rebecca and she has a strong Chicago accent, which forces me to ask how someone born and raised here got into City.

'I just decided one day that I wanted to follow English football,' Rebecca answers. 'A British friend mailed me a United jersey so I decided I'd watch them, but for some reason it just didn't feel right. Then I travelled to Manchester and that's when it really caught fire. I knew I was City. City just felt right!'

A few days before I arrived in Chicago 13 people were killed in a mass shooting of the sort that is becoming all too common here. I'm haunted by the news from a city where more people were wounded and killed by gunfire this year than in Syria.

I broach the subject gently. The arguments that follow, though differing, are heated, passionate and well-informed. I choose to sit back and listen to the overall tone of the arguments.

No one seems to agree on a single root cause but theories range from segregation versus industrial segregation, strategically built freeways separating the classes, drugs, and the city's inability to adapt to and shift from an industrialized city to a next-generation 'first city', not 'second city'.

One thing becomes clear during the spirited debate: these people absolutely love their city and believe in it. Another thing is also clear at the end of the political discourse: Warren Garlick of Oldham is *not* in the mood for political discourse.

'Lads, we've just done United 4-1; no more political talk – let's just enjoy this!' he pleads.

He isn't trying to sweep Chicago's problems under the rug; rather Warren knows the importance of a time and place. And today we're in The Globe. And we've just beaten United.

Chicago

It's 2.30pm and we're cruising through Wicker Park in the back of a yellow cab on what is now officially a drunken Sunday afternoon. On our way to the restaurant, Andrew and Mark begin to argue over whose bagels are better, New York's or Montreal's. I've got to side with Mark and go Montreal on this one – you know something is good when two Ontario boys argue in favour of Montreal.

The banter is lighthearted, and combined with my slight buzz and the passing breeze kindly finding its way into my ear through the rolled down window, it creates the perfect soundtrack for a warm afternoon drive through Wicker Park.

The food scene in Chicago is second to none, and as I sit on the patio of Big Star, a taco restaurant owned by Michelin-starred chef Paul Kahan, I am thoroughly convinced of this fact. Pastor tacos, fish tacos, walking tacos (which substitute their shell for a bag of Fritos Corn Chips and oh my God holy shit are they good), three shots of whisky and a pitcher of Schlitz beer resting in front of us. This would be heaven after a 4-1 *loss* to United. The derby win is the secret sauce on what is already the best meal I've ever had.

This day can't get any better, but it is about to get complicated.

I'm not supposed to drink whisky. It's been a while, and as the demon brew sits a tantalizing arm's length from my lips, I quietly mull over my decision for a few moments before concluding, 'Fuck it, I'll just have one.' I down the shot and no sooner does its warmth reach my belly than my phone beeps. I have a text message. And it is exactly who I'm afraid it is.

'Guess who is the proud owner of a new Manchester City hoodie?' the text reads. The text is of course from Natasha. Could this woman possibly send a more suggestive text on derby day? I mean, come on! I tell the lads my situation; I have a girlfriend back home whom I love dearly and it has been a long-distance situation for the better part of two years. We are absolutely committed to one another, no questions there.

I then tell them about Friday night and meeting Natasha. Mark, being my age and a divorced father of two understands the dilemma completely. Andrew, on the other hand, not so much. We have another beer and some more tacos; tacos de panza, taco de papas con rajas, each bite better than the one before. Mark and I espouse our drunken mid-30s 'knowledge' of life and women to young Andrew, who can't wrap his head around why seeing Natasha might be a bad decision.

We explain that life starts to get really great around your late 20s, before getting super-complicated by your early 30s, a window we all agree is cruelly short-lived. You won't have it figured out by your mid-30s, you'll just be too tired most of the time to make the sorts of mistakes you used to; this is what we attempt to convince young Andrew is true. It isn't that men grow wiser, we just become mercifully lazier.

It is now 3.30pm and Mark needs to get going. He invites me back to his place later in the evening for movies and more beer. This is exactly what I *should* do, but instead I politely decline and know there will be a decision to make back at my hotel.

By the time the taxi drops me at the hotel, my texting with Natasha has resulted in a dinner invitation. It's an invitation I would love to accept. I'd like to shower up, put on a nicer shirt and maybe some cologne. I want to go out with Natasha on a Saturday night in Chicago and see more of this intoxicating city. I want adventure. The Kabanes, champagne, local craft beer, the whisky – hell even the Schlitz – begin to swirl around inside my head and cloud my better judgement. I'm not thinking clearly until I'm not thinking at all. I am 36 years old and before I can make the sort of mistake someone Andrew Tripp's age might, I pass out, face down on my hotel room bed.

I come to sometime around 6pm, feeling every sip of my two-day drink fest. I text Natasha back and tell her I have too much writing due to meet up tonight – which I suddenly realize is *true,* as I still haven't filed my monthly blog for City – shit! Natasha writes back, 'How about breakfast?' and while it sounds a much safer option, it's a decision I'll wrestle with tomorrow on a clear head and a clean conscience.

It's 10.55am on an absolutely picture-perfect September Monday in downtown Chicago. I'm walking down Ohio Street searching for a well-known Illinois breakfast chain called Yolk and as I draw nearer my stomach feels just the way it does before a derby kicks off. I no longer miss the nervous excitement you get when meeting someone new. I feel instead conflicted and entirely uncomfortable. I should just go to the airport, phone Jess, eat a bad departure lounge croissant and drink a five-dollar orange juice. I was pretty drunk when I met Natasha and there is part of me hoping she isn't as beautiful as I recall. When I finally find the restaurant, Natasha is waiting by the entrance and she is even more beautiful in the sober light of day.

Over eggs Benedict I listen to and watch Natasha, enthralled by her stylish dress and radiantly carved cheekbones as she tells me of growing up in Croatia, moving to the States at seventeen, studying law and becoming a lawyer at one of the largest firms in the country. In her free time she helps young offenders convicted as adults to gain early release from prison. She tells me about her favourite client, and his story is similar to one I need for a screenplay I've been chipping away at. Perhaps we should stay in touch for this reason, I try telling myself.

Natasha admits to phoning her father yesterday, a massive footy fan back home in Croatia, and asking him who Manchester City are. He told her, 'They're a very big club now, but it wasn't always that way.'

As Natasha describes her new City jumper ordered online and her condo just across the street, I imagine us sharing breakfast together there, her wearing the pink City jumper and little else. I imagine us drinking expensive coffee, even though I don't drink coffee, and discussing world events and where we might go for dinner. I picture us in bed together with a view of the Lakeshore Path, and joggers.

After breakfast, Natasha offers to walk me to the L Train instead of taking another cab, cars being completely contrary to the carbon footprint discussion we enjoyed over post-breakfast cups of tea. As Natasha guides me through the streets of this one-of-a-kind metropolis – burned down and built back up again during the art deco era – proudly showing off her new home, I think that a man could live a thousand lives and never have a more elegant tour guide in a more breathtaking city.

We take a detour so we can pass by the Tribune Tower, a building she tells me is, 'My favourite and most romantic building in the city.' When she realizes she's called the building 'romantic' Natasha immediately backpedals, 'I didn't mean romantic in that way, I mean we're not making out against the side of the building,' she says. I laugh and wonder how much of that is true.

Then Natasha shares a subject we have both, until now, managed to avoid. She is recently out of a tough relationship and unsure if she and her ex can work things out this time around. I know this is the appropriate time to own up to my relationship status. I subtly work in that my girlfriend and I, too, went through a rough patch, but we're better for it now and perhaps this will happen in her case. Things feel right having said that and we both take the knowledge of one another's relationship status in our stride. In fact, we don't miss a beat and, if anything, the conversation only continues to get better.

A Mexican gentleman stops us as I take a picture of the Tribune building. He takes notice of my City shirt and wants to talk footy, so we do for a bit. It seems as though everyone in the world watched yesterday's derby and it feels both strange and wonderful to be on the winning side. I tell Natasha she can expect this sort of random conversation with strangers once her new City jumper arrives. Natasha and I part ways at the subway entrance with a quick kiss on the cheek and an embrace just long enough to confirm her looks and scent are a perfect match.

For a few short hours I was fortunate enough to have a beautiful woman as my personal chaperone around a world-class city. Natasha and I texted back and forth for a few more days, until eventually we didn't. I haven't heard from her since, and that's probably the best way for things to be left.

As I leave Chicago by way of the Orange Line to Midway airport, one final landmark catches my eye. My gaze is drawn out the window towards a working-class suburb of Chicago, somewhere between Kedzie and Pulaski stations. There in the distance, I see it. In someone's front yard sitting proudly, brightly, magnificently. A bouncy castle. And I'm reminded of what really brought me here and of the journey's first true success. I chuckle a bit as I think to myself,

'You lucky bastard.'

5
LOS ANGELES

First Impressions

THE FIRST time I flew in to Los Angeles I was 20 years old. My band was on a connecting flight to Australia, when our then-idiot-drummer thought he had a shot with some girl that lived out here (he didn't) and somehow convinced us to endure an eight-hour layover at LAX. To no great surprise, the girl never showed and the first eight hours of my LA experience were spent in the airport.

Two things remain in my memory from late 1990s Los Angeles. The first one is stepping outside the terminal so our bass player could smoke, and laying eyes on my first ever palm tree. The other was coming in to land and the way Los Angeles looked from above.

To my small-town Canadian eyes the city appeared every bit the frightening slum depicted in the films of my youth. All the homes appeared yellowed, the spaces separating them narrow and the roads, as we grew closer to them, cracked and neglected. More simply put, at the age of 20 I knew nothing of Los Angeles. If you could go back in time, sit beside that 20-year-old kid, as he peered ignorantly out of the plane's window, and tell him that 12 years later he would call this place home, he'd have told you you were nuts. But 12 years later I would call Los Angeles home, Los Feliz to be exact. And 15 years later, on approach to LAX, I don't see a frightening slum, I see familiar landmarks. For me, the Griffith Observatory stands out more than the Hollywood sign, and the palm trees, no longer strange and exotic, their familiar leaves now serving as old friends waving 'welcome back'.

LA is easily one of the most misunderstood cities in the world. Too many people only experience this city as a tourist, and the tourist's version is a wholly different one to that of a resident. If you haven't been to LA yet, I strongly suggest connecting with a local as your guide, and if you don't know anyone in LA, perhaps this chapter can help. Los Angeles is one of the world's great cities and I'll argue that with anyone who feels like doing so at El Compadre, over a bottle of Victoria and some fish tacos.

My love for this city shocks those who knew me in my youth. Back then, I was very much the flag-waving, anti-American, Captain Canada type, but travel is this world's great equalizer. Journey to almost any place, meet the right people and you'll be hard-pressed to hate anywhere.

I fly into Los Angeles two weeks early to spend time with my old friends and it proves a rewarding decision. My old writers gang – Larry, Aña Lisa, their daughter, Scarlett, and Ron Anderson – throw me a touching Canadian Thanksgiving dinner complete with Canadian flag bunting around the circumference of their cozy Burbank dining room. I go to a Kings hockey game, the Dodgers' play-off game four, eat at all of my favourite Mexican restaurants at least twice and generally have the kind of great time that makes me wish I still lived here.

I catch up with my former room-mate Liz, an excommunicated Mormon who rented me my first apartment. I have lunch with Norman, who was proud to hear I was finally pursuing his urgings to work on a book. Fellow wordsmiths Jaime and Ronnie join me for beers in West Hollywood, a pair so quick-witted you become a better writer just by virtue of their proximity. If you become a writer for only one reason, getting to sit around and drink with fellow writers is as good a reason as any.

And then there's Jason Carvey.

If you wondered where I'm sleeping for the majority of these three weeks, well here it is: I'm staying with a Red bastard. One of my best friends in the world is putting me up on his couch in Echo Park, just as he has countless times before, and as I have done for him in Toronto, Manchester, and Oxfordshire – we won't get into Oxfordshire.

I first met Jason Carvey when he came up to Toronto to shoot a music video for my band. He and his two other crewmembers, Bruce and Todd, booked themselves into one of the swankiest boutique hotels in Toronto – a room in which Jason spent exactly one hour of his three-day visit.

The rest were spent in absolute squalor crashing on my stain-riddled indie-music sofa at 214 Brunswick Avenue. They remain three of the best and most important days of my life.

Sadly, Jason's mate Darren played in the United youth squad of the early 1990s and got his hooks into Carvey before I could turn him Blue. I'll forgive Jason his sins; he was, after all, just a young impressionable American, not the first nor the last to fall victim to the red side of Trafford.

I take the LAX flyaway bus to the airport which is within 15 minutes of Redondo Beach, where I am to meet my host for the weekend. I'm about two steps off the bus at Terminal 7 when I hear a bone-chilling, hooligan-esque 'Oi!' I turn to discover a stocky Manc in his early 40s with a shaved head, waiting by a truck with 'MCFC LA' licence plates and a vicious-looking dog in the back. This is Tim Bramley and he definitely appears on the surface to be the hardest Blue I've met yet.

Fuck, I was worried this was going to happen. I can't keep meeting the friendliest supporters the world over; at some point my chaperone was destined to be some brawler from the wrong side of Stockport and now as I walk towards Tim's truck I'm certain this day has arrived. I'm terrified about what might happen if he finds out I've only been a Blue for ten years or that I was once filmed with my band – though quite literally kicking and screaming – outside of Old Trafford.

If a geezer such as Tim were to learn of this, surely I'd be a dead man. 'Imposter!' he'd shout as an army of steel-toed youth quickly emerged from the shadows to deliver their worst. Best to keep these incriminating anecdotes to myself, I decide.

I step into the truck and Tim's part-boxer, part-bulldog, part-pitbull, Charlie, quickly licks the back of my neck; despite the alarming mix of breeds, he is harmless.

As we make the short drive from El Segundo to Tim's gaff in Redondo Beach, he rings up a cabbie he claims to know and the conversation is a riot. I don't need to know what the cabbie on the other end is saying to figure out he has little clue who Tim is or how he got his personal mobile number. Tim on the other hand could not be more sing-songy in his friendliness, to the point of almost harassing the poor man.

'Of course you know me, mate, it's Tim, I know your brother, pal,' Tim assures him in a playful Stockport accent. 'Well then tell your brother to come get us, mate; I'll need a ride in about five minutes… no, 20 minutes won't do, mate. Tell you what, make it 15 and that'll give us time for a quick beer before we go.'

Five minutes later we pull into a gorgeous little home near the ocean, head inside for a quick Blue Moon, change our shirts, and when the cabbie's brother arrives right on time, Tim states assertively, 'It's time to get fucking going!'

Inside of ten minutes we're at the famous Hermosa pier and settling in to a pint at Silvio's, a small Brazilian bar on the strip. For those who haven't been to Hermosa Beach it is filled with what your most favourable stereotypes of Los Angeles probably are: palm trees and attractive people wearing very little clothing, set against the backdrop of the Pacific Ocean.

It doesn't take long to realize Tim knows just about everybody. We sit down for happy hour at about 5.30pm and are quickly joined by Chris Wode, who looks a lot like the actor Robert Patrick, the man who played T-1000 in *Terminator 2*. In fact, Wodey looks so much like him that I briefly entertain the thought that he may very well be Robert Patrick – after all, this is LA – before quickly remembering Robert Patrick must be a good 15 years older than Wodey. Still, wearing mirrored aviator shades and chomping on a toothpick between his teeth, the resemblance, it must be said, is remarkable.

Paul Lyons joins us next. Paul is a part-owner of Silvio's and gives Tim and I the heads-up that the local IPA we're drinking has a bit of a kick to it. Less than two hours into my visit, I find myself hanging out with lads who refer to Rod Stewart as 'Rod' and tell stories about a mate named 'Manny' who, as it turns out, is none other than Manny of Stone Roses fame. I know I'm in for a good night here.

Originally from Reddish, Tim grew up best mates with Mark 'amore' Wood from our Toronto Blues and as with any old friendship, it's time to take the piss out of poor Woody for a bit. The teasing starts with Tim making fun of how little Woody can drink, the nickname 'Two Bud Wood' not unfamiliar to either of us. But I carry a dark secret in this regard; Woody and I share the same tolerance for alcohol, which is – as you are beginning to learn – not a great deal. Better keep this from Tim for the time being as well.

After more pints than I can count, we head over to George Best's old bar, which he opened back in his LA Aztecs playing days. There is a small line of people outside when we arrive, one that we march straight past, the same way I'm sure Tim did in his Hacienda days. Hanging out with these lads has somehow caused The Charlatans' 'Can't Get Out of Bed' to begin playing inside my head, and every step I take is now a confident strut. This is also where the night begins to get a bit fuzzy.

I know we were at Best's old place, which I *think* is now called The Underground. I know I had a Boddingtons, perhaps two. I feel like Wodey came with us and then disappeared without telling anyone. I know Paul made it all the way to the pizza joint with Tim and myself, yet I'm sure more people were there with us. I remember commandeering a pizza from a waiter destined for another table – or as the lads would later debate, stole a pizza from a customer picking up his takeaway order.

I know we took a cab back to Tim's and I like to imagine it was the cabbie's brother again, but at this point I'm only guessing. We definitely finished the night, or morning I suppose, at Tim's, scarfing down homemade tofu curry he left simmering on the stovetop all day, curry that was absolutely luscious, that much I know for sure. I met Tim's wife, Candy, and I can only hope her first impression of me wasn't that of a ravenous and drunk Canadian dribbling curry down the front of his shirt. Evidence the next morning suggests I tried reading a book before passing out and sent a text message to someone called Tato, which simply read, 'El Canadiense!'

What a dick.

If Chicago's hangover was a nine-out-of-ten and ten is death, then Tim and the lads have managed to saddle me with something in the neighbourhood of a 12. Certainly death would be preferable to this. Good thing City has the late match today – 9.30am. You might think eating half a stolen pizza and a bowl of homemade curry would help stave off a hangover, but you would be mistaken. What the hell was in that IPA?

Saturday 19 October. West Ham v City. 9.30am kick-off

Candy, Tim and I arrive at On The Rocks, 239 North Harbor Drive, Redondo Beach, around 8.45am for West Ham versus Manchester City. On The Rocks is quite literally *on* the rocks that separate venue from ocean, but the view from outside the pub which is idyllic, serene, magnificent, all that good stuff, does very little to ease my pain. Once inside however, no matter how picturesque its surroundings, a pub at 9am is still a pub at 9am, anywhere in the world; LA's unique twist is an aroma of stale beer and ocean air.

The layout of LA, the traffic, and Manchester City's ever-increasing popularity have resulted in two MCFC

Official Supporters Clubs here in Los Angeles, and today's match is made even more special because the two clubs will be watching this match together, the Hollywood Blues battling their way along La Brea, perhaps La Cienega, and almost certainly the 405 to get to Redondo Beach in time for a 9.30am kick-off.

Tim arrives at our table with two Bloody Marys. He and I likely drank the same amount last night, yet here Tim is a few hours later fresh as a goddamned daisy. The next two Blues through the door help me feel a little better about myself. If misery loves company, then here comes company. Wodey saddles up to the table in his aviators, but instead of looking like T-1000 as he did yesterday, he looks more like a traffic cop who's been to Tijuana and back.

'You feeling as wretched as I am?' I ask.

'Dude, I don't remember the end of the night *at all*.'

And it isn't just the North Americans in rough shape this morning. Paul Lyons staggers through the door – after much speculation he wouldn't – and quickly confesses, 'Lads, I woke up with my lips stuck to my teeth.'

There is a measure of camaraderie that comes with a hangover; we're in this one together and that helps ease the pain, if only slightly. Tim, who I'm now convinced is impervious to the effects of alcohol, brings more drinks over to the table, before I've even had a chance to say no to the first round. I don't want to offend my host, but there is no way I'll get another sip of alcohol down me without vomiting. I pull out my phone and text Woody for advice.

Text to Woody, *'I'm not sure what happened last night but I drank a hell of a lot more than I should have and now Tim is trying to force more booze down me. Can I say no? Will he get offended? What's my call here?'*

Text from Woody, *'We call that the Tim factor!'*

Cheers Woody, absolutely no help at all, mate.

The next Blue to stroll in from the beachfront is Adam Pomfret, better known as Pommy. Another Reddish Blue, luckily Pommy is more into Iron Man events and healthy living than he is encouraging morning drinking. Pommy – who is also from this mythical place they call Reddish – arrived in Los Angeles in May of 2000 and his story is a familiar one amongst the expats here in Los Angeles; he fell in love with a woman, then the weather, and he never looked back.

As Pommy tells it, his wife, Janette, is the daughter of an ex-United player who, in the 1960s, moved to Boston and became a ringer in a peculiar era of semi-professional soccer in Massachusetts. Eventually Adam's father-in-law took a job in California and that's where the family settled. A year after Pommy's wedding, Tim Bramley came for a visit and fell in love with Janette's best friend, then the weather, before he too decided LA was the place for him.

So here they are, two lads from Reddish, one a former cop, the other very much not a former cop, the hard days of Reddish behind them, enjoying a new and much warmer life here in Los Angeles.

We're seven matches into the new campaign, and City's away form has been poor thus far. Brilliant at the Etihad, City have only managed one point from a possible nine away from the familiar confines of East Manchester. West Ham, on the other hand, are on surprisingly good form to start their campaign and are coming off a 3-0 drubbing of their rivals Spurs, away at White Hart Lane no less. So when Sergio Aguero puts us up 15 minutes into the affair, the nerves settle enough for me to enjoy a bit of an omelette and home fries, which have arrived at the table courtesy of a motherly Candy.

By half-time, the ice in my untouched Bloody Mary has long since melted and Tim mercifully replaces it with a

Corona. That I can handle. Within minutes of the restart, Sergio knocks in a textbook header, one I admittedly miss while chatting with Wodey about his days on a soccer scholarship at the University of Greensboro, where he used to blast Oasis before a match, the band who got him into City serving up the pre-match soundtrack on a small campus in North Carolina.

West Ham pull one back a few minutes later but it barely registers; City are sublime today, the away jinx is nowhere to be seen and the Blues in Redondo Beach appear more content to mix and mingle than stress about the three points. Just for good measure David Silva reminds the Hammers we are a far tougher opponent than Tottenham and puts City up two goals to the good; final score, City 3, Hammers 1, a much-needed three points on the road secured.

The post-match affair at On The Rocks is far from a piss-up. Here, families and a healthy lifestyle rule the day and it's a nice change of pace, to be honest. There is little doubt in my mind that Tim was not someone to be messed with back in Reddish, hell Adam and Paul probably weren't saints either. But Los Angeles seems to have peeled away a layer of defence no longer needed by these three men from England's northern capital, all seemingly at ease living along California's southern coast.

After the final whistle, the Hollywood and Redondo Blues head outside for a group photo, balanced on the jagged rocks that protect their local pub from their local ocean, before adjourning to the back patio for buckets of Corona.

Here, I am joined by a trio of Hollywood Blues: Paul Carnall, Bernadette Gilbey and Matthew Kershaw, who started the Hollywood Blues just hours before the QPR match in 2012.

'We met on the official supporters message boards and discovered we were all about to watch the finals alone,' Matthew explains. So with only hours to spare before City's biggest match in most of our lifetimes, Matthew Kershaw, a South African expat; Paul Carnal, a Wiganer who came to LA on vacation, fell in love and never left; and Bernadette, the born-and-raised Californian, decided to meet at Fox and Hounds – an Arsenal pub. There, with 75 Gooners cheering them on, the new friends watched and cheered as City claimed their first league title in 44 years.

As Paul regales us all with romantic memories of Third Division football, I feel another set of suspicious eyes on me. In the back corner of On The Rocks's patio sit two Hispanic gentlemen each wearing home City tops. One shirt is last season's home blue, the other a Thomas Cook-era shirt with 'Vassell' printed across the back. Both men keep their heads shaved pretty near to the scalp and both wear dark and rather menacing sunglasses. What's worse is they appear to be sizing me up, perhaps wondering what the hell I'm doing here and why I'm asking so many questions.

Tough and unapproachable looks aside, I know I must approach their table and ask how this intimidating duo came to support City. Before heading over, I remind myself of the time I was on the LA subway, sitting across from a Hispanic gentleman absolutely covered in tattoos. It was one of my first rides on the LA Metro and I was scared I might get off at the wrong stop and wind up in this dude's neighbourhood. Upon closer inspection, I discovered Morrissey badges covering the entirety of his leather satchel. I instantly went from guarded to wanting to ask him which he considered a better album: *Vauxhall and I* or *Your Arsenal*. Looks can be deceiving; we judge too quickly. I need to remind myself of this as I get up the courage to ask two shady-looking strangers why they support the same football club as I do. I approach the table and nervously introduce myself to Isaac Valaga and Michael Torres.

'How did you guys get into City?' I ask.

'He got me into City,' Isaac answers, pointing to Michael, who wears the Darius Vassell top.

'So how did you get into City?' I ask Michael.

'Oasis.'

Four cities into my tour and Oasis are the overwhelming answer to how most Americans came to support Manchester City. I don't think Mancunians fully grasp just how revered their music is in major cities the world over, or what a major impact Manchester as a whole continues to have on global culture. For a city of less than one million people it is far beyond remarkable, and I'm certain there's something in the water.

Beside Michael and Isaac, bouncing a toddler on his knee, sits Michael's father Ruben Torres. Ruben came to California from Mexico and instilled a love of Mexican football in his son. Many years later, during the dramatics of 2012's final match, Michael, along with some help from Sergio Aguero, instilled a love of Manchester City in Ruben. Ruben now watches every City match, and on this day proudly displays the City badge with 'Champions 2012' stitched on the front of his polo shirt. The toddler on Ruben's knee is his grandson, Michael's son Mason. Mason wears the infant version of last year's home kit and as an added feature, has his name Mason and the number one printed across the back.

'Take a look at this,' Michael says, excitedly pulling out his mobile. 'I'm making this for Mason.' Displayed on Michael's phone is a giant City badge carved from wood, easily three feet by three feet.

'I'm going to put this in his room when it's finished.'

And just like that, in five short minutes, I've gone from intimidated by strangers to jealous of a two-year-old.

If Los Angeles is a misunderstood city, then its Hispanic citizens – who make up nearly 50 per cent of the population – are its misunderstood heartbeat. In a city so richly steeped in and linked to film and television, Hispanics are too often represented as the villains, or thugs. I'm glad I approached Michael today; I'm thankful he was here. Meetings such as these are a powerful reminder of why travel is so important.

Bernadette Gilbey, the born-and-raised California girl, tells one of the more incredible tales of how she found her way to Manchester City. You would be forgiven for thinking it sounds too good to be, but if this is indeed how Bernadette's heart turned Blue, then it is the best argument yet for why Oasis are one of City's all-time greatest ambassadors and a clear front-runner for my favourite story of how someone became a City supporter, even if in the end there are some Hollywood liberties in her telling.

'It was 1994 and I was in Brighton and my friend and I were on tour with the band Suede,' Bernadette begins.

'Wow, I used to love Suede. What were you doing on tour with them?' I ask.

'We were just friends with them.'

'Yeah, but how? Were you working on the tour as well?'

'Look, when you're an attractive young woman attending UCLA and you want to meet a band, it isn't a hard thing to do,' Bernadette says curtly, and I know to leave it there.

'My friend and I were really into Oasis at the time; they'd just put out their first album. We couldn't get tickets and the boys in Suede didn't know them, but their management knew them and told us about a pub where the band might be ahead of their show in Brighton.

'Sure enough as we sat drinking a pint in this tiny little pub, in strolls Noel Gallagher. He sits down next to us and asks, "Where are you girls from?" We tell him we're from California and after a bit of light conversation we come clean and admit that we really want to go to his concert, but don't have any tickets.

'Noel points to a tiny TV in the corner of the pub and says, "You see that team in blue up there? That's my team. If you sit here with me and watch the entire match, I'll give you both tickets for the show tonight." For the next two hours I watched my first-ever Manchester City match with Noel Gallagher proudly explaining the entire history of his club. At the end of the match Noel got up to leave and simply told us, "City are your club now." And I was like, hell yeah, this is my club!'

And sitting here nearly 20 years later, whether this is how it happened or not, Manchester City remains Bernadette Gilbey's one and only team.

One Hollywood Blue absent from today's trip to Redondo Beach is Ian MacLeod. At this moment Ian is in a hospital room where he will spend 70 days waging war on cancer. By the time this season ends Ian will be in remission and will film a video crediting his fellow Blues for giving him the 'Pride In Battle' necessary to attack his disease. City supporters will vote Ian's, the Story of the Year on an online platform known as 'CityStories'. The club and CityStories will subsequently reward Ian with his first trip to the Etihad.

Los Angeles

After a few hours on the back patio, Tim and I decide to hit the beach. I swim off some of my hangover in the Pacific Ocean and get my ass handed to me in a beanbag game called Baggo. It was pretty even, until I over-celebrated my Hail Mary shot for the win. Tim put his foot on the gas after that and I didn't win another round. After a good swim and Baggo, we set up two chairs and watch the tide – among other things. Tim and I sneak a cheeky glance at a few girls playing beach volleyball. When the girls catch us having our little peek, we both quickly turn our heads back to the ocean and giggle at being caught.

'Not bad for a kid from Toronto and a lad from Reddish, eh?' I say, as we watch the waves, one after the other, make gentle landfall in Southern California.

'Peaceful innit,' Tim comments, in his relaxed and charming Reddish tone.

'Sure beats wailing car alarms.'

'You know the thing I don't miss about Manchester?' Tim asks. 'Having me fucking car stolen.'

'When did you have your car stolen?' I ask.

'Mate, I've had *two* stolen! After my first motor was nicked I bought a nice red Lexus with the cash from the insurance. Well, it wasn't long after that, my house was broken into and the bastards got my spare set of keys. When the cops came round they asked me if they got anything else, and I told them, "My extra set of car keys!" "Oh, they'll definitely be back for that Lexus then," was the cops' answer. So I asked them, "What are you going to do about it then?" They just rolled their eyes at me and said, "Well we don't have the manpower to wait for them outside your house now do we?"

'I told them they'd be coming back later in the night to investigate a murder, and I was dead serious, mate. I chained the front gate shut, with the car inside, grabbed me bat and waited for the bastards to return.

'And then I promptly fell fast asleep. The sun woke me up at 7am and I jumped to the window, pulled back the curtain, found the gate off its hinges and my Lexus gone. Don't miss that about back home.'

Tim takes a few moments, staring back out at the ocean, and as serene and tranquil as the Pacific is, and despite having had two cars stolen, I can still see a man who misses home at the mention of his Manchester.

'You know I learned my father died on my wedding day. He didn't die on my wedding day, I only found out on my wedding day. We were estranged, you see,' Tim confides.

His statement comes out of thin air, but then the ocean can have this effect on people. There is also something about watching football together, the bond between supporters that has the mysterious ability to open up the hearts of even the hardest men.

And as we sit here watching the tide, I am beginning to understand the word 'supporter' carries a lot more weight than I may have realized. I also realize that the man I initially thought might be the hardest I've met is anything but. This man who looked like a hooligan is a kind and generous host who loves his wife, and his dog, and *Star Trek*. And he loves his new home, a place that like his old home, is so often misunderstood.

As we sit there in our lawn chairs stuck into the sand, the sun slowly begins to disappear behind the rippling salt water.

'Hey Tim, does the tide come in or out at night?' I ask.

'Don't know, mate. All I know is, it's something to do with the moon.'

We wrap the night up just as you'd expect a once-brawler from Reddish and mild-mannered Canadian pizza thief would on a Saturday in Los Angeles. I eat watermelon and fall asleep on the couch while Tim drinks a Blue Moon and watches the latest *Star Trek* film.

6
DALLAS

Red, Blue and Barbecue

OKAY, SO we aren't technically in Dallas yet and we may not get there. I had a feeling there would be cities planned that got missed along the way, and Dallas may well prove to be the first.

I'm at Los Angeles international airport, about 20 minutes away from boarding a US Airways flight to Dallas, Texas, by way of Phoenix, Arizona. I'm at the departure gate and I've scrolled through every social media page, read my text messages, and exhausted all my apps – except for one.

I know I *should* check my banking app, I just haven't been able to bring myself to do so. I know I *should* have about $300 left on my credit card, an amount that would easily see me through two nights in Dallas before flying home to Toronto and starting work for two months. But the nagging voice in the back of my head, the one reminding me I went out for goodbye drinks with Jason Carvey last night, finally convinces me to check the balance. Just in case. I log on to my banking app and peer nervously through squinting eyes: *Available credit: $0.00.*

My heart instantly sinks to the bottom of my stomach. Forgot about those pesky monthly interest charges, didn't I.

'This is a pre-boarding announcement for US Airways flight 437 with service to Phoenix...'

Oh. Shit.

I desperately tear through my bag, maybe there's some miracle stash of money I've forgotten about? Aha, I can feel some bills!

$4.30.

You make strange decisions when you're down to your last four dollars. I figure I've got about 20 minutes to sort this out. Knowing I'm hungry, knowing I'm broke and knowing my flight is going to leave within the half-hour, what do I do? I search for a cheap souvenir for Jess. To date I've brought Jess a tiny souvenir from each city, and my first thought becomes, 'Shit, I can't break the streak!'

I quickly realize LA's trinket is going to have to take a pass, then rush to McDonald's and order a value-menu cheeseburger with extra pickles (because somehow if I alter my order, have them custom-make me something off-menu I'm not desperately eating at McDonald's). One bite into their famous 'cheeseburger' and the urgency is fully realized, 'I need money!'

Less than a year ago I was the co-owner of a decent little sports business. Now I am a 36-year-old unemployed writer, about to call his father for a loan.

My father is one of the most reliable men on the planet. I can see him back at home with his morning cup of coffee and an English muffin with jam as he watches his favourite morning show, *Kelly and Michael*. My dad answers on the third ring. Is he happy to help? No. Does he help? Yes. Is he still proud of me? Strangely, he is.

My dad fronts me $200. I don't feel great about it, but I'm back on my feet. Fearing the banks will somehow take that money instantly and arbitrarily put it into some overdue account I owe ungodly amounts of interest on, I immediately sprint to the ATM nearest my gate. I frantically punch in my four-digit code, peeking over my shoulder at the disappearing line of fellow passengers and holding my breath. The sound and the feeling of $200 cascading out from the cash machine is on par with winning a Lucky-7s slot machine and I promise myself that if I'm ever fortunate enough to make a bit of money in this life, I will *never* forget what an incredible sum of money 200 dollars can be.

I board the plane to Dallas, which will connect via Phoenix. I'll have $200 burning a hole in my pocket, my hotel room in Dallas has already been taken care of, and in two days' time I'll be back in Canada with two months of full-time work ahead of me. It looks like part one of this adventure might just go off without a hitch.

By the time I meet up with the storm, we are somewhere just outside of Fort Worth; Abilene maybe? The ominous clouds that were in the distance only a few minutes ago now surround us, the rain, wind and thunder, now slamming against our tiny vessel, lightning striking in every direction, as we desperately scramble for safety. It is clear to me that we won't be landing in Dallas; I just hope we're going to land somewhere. Whilst I squirm nervously in my seat, the pilots expertly navigate us around the giant storm and land us safely – in Houston. If I was nervous for a moment, it is nothing compared to a landing I'll experience a few months from now.

The pilot tells us he's leaning towards a plan to re-fuel and get us back up to Dallas as soon as they lift the ground stop. I sure hope this happens, because I am still relatively penniless, it's approaching 9pm and my hotel is booked for Dallas, not Houston. Not to mention City versus Chelsea kicks off at 11am and I'll never get into Dallas in time if we don't leave tonight.

As I stare out from the tiny window at the runway, watching a young ground crewman impress his colleague by jumping from a standing position on to the top of a concrete barrier about four feet off the ground, over and over again, I am struck with the strange memory that people used to clap on planes. I recall being 18 years old and flying from Toronto into Glasgow, and when the plane touched down everyone on board applauded, grateful for what we had just experienced, transatlantic travel in less than seven hours.

I feel like I remember a few flights back in those days ending the same way until one day they just didn't. The sound of applause replaced by tired groans and hands scrambling for cellphones rather than against one another in appreciation. I decide that if we get into Dallas tonight, I'm doing it. I will bring back the applause.

Nearly two hours pass and all I can hear in my head is the theme music from *Planes, Trains and Automobiles*. I'm tired. I want a bed. I'm starving and I want Dallas barbecue. I want three points from Chelsea in the morning and then I want to go home. Just as I convince myself I'll be sleeping in the Houston airport and missing Dallas all together the captain comes over the PA, 'If we're going to go, it has to be right now.'

'Seat tables in the upright positions, seatbelts on and shut those phones off, or we're all sleeping on the floor of George Bush International Airport,' adds the head flight attendant. Did I mention the airport in Houston is named George Bush International? Turn your damn phones off people and let's get to Dallas!

Ninety minutes later we touch down at Dallas Fort Worth airport and before I can take the lead, the passengers applaud a job well done by our much more exhausted US Airways flight 551 crew. Their shifts were technically over three hours ago and they could easily have left us in Houston as tomorrow's problem. This chapter exists because they exist. At 2am I finally check into my hotel near Dallas Forth Worth airport, order up a late-night pizza and catch a few hours' sleep.

Dallas, Texas

The next morning, as I stand in the hotel lobby watching planes fly into the world's third-busiest airport, one after the other, I feel like Ebenezer Scrooge by the time he reaches the third ghost. I know a new stranger is coming for me, I just have no idea who they will be, nor what they will be like.

As my eyes trace a 747 floating gracefully towards the runway, a shiny new Honda Accord squeals up to the entrance of the Dallas Fort Worth Sheraton. Its windows are tinted and I can't see inside. Is this my ride? What sort of Blue awaits me this time?

The driver's door opens even before the car is fully stopped and out jumps Mark Mulvanny, a short and stocky gentleman in his late 30s. Mark reminds me of a younger (think *Long Good Friday*) Bob Hoskins with a few tins of Red Bull in him. The man runs around the back of his still-running car and before even asking if I am who he thinks I am – though my Aguero top likely tips him off – wraps me in a giant bear hug and lifts me off the ground.

'Welcome to Dallas, mate!' Mark shouts.

As we make the 25-mile drive to Frisco, Texas, where Blue Moon Dallas assembles, I notice Mark's accent leans more to the Mancunian side than it does the Texan. Mark explains to me that he moved to the States from Manchester 28 years ago, arriving in New York and then moving onward to Texas after university, never fully losing his Mancunian inflection; a shame, as I've been looking forward to hearing Texan accents talk about Manchester City. But I needn't worry, that's on the way.

In the back seat of Mark's fully loaded Honda sits his eight-year-old lad called Bubba (of course), quietly playing video games on his iPad. Bubba appears shy. I would be, too, if my dad had just picked up some strange transient footy fan at nine in the morning. Mark tries to involve Bubba in our conversation by asking him to share what he's watching on his tablet. I get the impression Bubba doesn't want to, but Mark insists. What follows plays out as though it were an uncomfortable scene from *The Office,* Mark fully reminding me of Ricky Gervais's character David Brent.

'What you looking at back there, Bubba?' Mark asks, before excitedly turning to me.

Bubba buries his head deeper into the tablet.

'Wait a minute that's not your…' Mark looks back at me, and *sotto voce* informs, 'He wants to show you his soccer videos.'

Brilliant, I think, Bubba has some favourite YouTube clips of City he watches before a match.

'Great idea Bubba, show me some goals then! You got Sergio on there?' I ask.

Bubba shakes his head to say no.

Mark turns his attention back to Bubba, 'Is that your…? Wait a minute, do you want to show Darryl *your* soccer video?' Mark again turns to me and I definitely feel like the cameraman in a documentary film.

'He's shy but he wants to show you his soccer video.'

Mark turns his head away from the road – it's worth mentioning we're on a roaring Texas freeway as this unfolds – and reaches back for Bubba's tablet.

'Go on then, Bubba, let us see these soccer videos.'

Feigning embarrassment, the proud dad passes me a tablet, not of YouTube videos, not of City, but of Bubba playing little-league soccer. As the video cues up, I begin to wonder if Mark thinks I might have some sort of influence with the Manchester City youth academy.

A few highlights into the video I begin to realize why Mark has pressed so hard to view the video. Bubba has the height and skill of kids three or four years his senior. He makes the other eight-year-olds look like toddlers by comparison and his natural skill set and techniques are as good as I've seen from most adults.

I've never said this of a kid before, and I hate to put undue pressure on what should be simple fun, but write this name down, folks. Bubba Bandit, real name Cameron Mulvanny. In about ten years' time, you just might be wearing it on the back of your replica kit.

Sunday 27 October. Chelsea v City. 11am kick-off

Twenty minutes and a netful of Bubba's highlight reel goals later, we arrive at The Londoner Pub, 5454 West Main Street in Frisco, Texas. The Londoner exists in the plaza next to FC Dallas's home stadium and I imagine on a matchday this area must be absolutely jam-packed. But this is 10.30am on a Sunday and we have the parking lot to ourselves. Mark pulls up right in front, pops the trunk and proudly presents me with my official Dallas Blues supporter's tee.

As we step inside The Londoner I find a pub equalled in beauty only by The Mad Hatter. The Hatter wins out by a nose, based on their gold-leaf City emblem, but apart from that not much separates these two pubs in terms of their aesthetic.

Halloween is only a few days away and it is a massive deal here in the United States. The Londoner reflects this with a surreal combination of hanging skeletons and vampire heads and an inflatable banana wearing a late-'80s-era City top, all resting directly under the Heart of the City award.

With a bit of time before kick-off I order myself some breakfast, making sure to add bacon, and it doesn't disappoint; Texas bacon was always going to be fantastic. The first Blue I get to know, after Mark, is Virgil Werley. They make 'em big in Texas and Virgil is no exception. With his ginger hair and soft-spoken approach, he looks like my brother-in-law might were he to consume human growth hormone. Virgil tells me the first great story of the day, and while it isn't about City, it draws a nice parallel and goes a long way in explaining why Virgil Werley chose to wear Blue.

'I used to go to Dallas Cowboy games all the time, before they became too expensive now that the new stadium is around,' he begins.

'We were getting killed by our arch rivals, the San Francisco 49ers. Their best player, Terrell Owens, scored a touchdown and ran straight to mid-field, celebrating on our giant star logo. The crowd went crazy. When he did it again after his next touchdown, the Cowboys' free-safety George Teague saw it coming. The whole crowd watched as he ran the length of the field, everyone but Terrell Owens knew he was coming, and we all went wild when he smashed him off our star in the middle of the field.'

Virgil takes a sip of his morning beer before concluding, 'I think that was the best loss I've ever been to.'

It reminds me of a great story Woody once told about City losing 5-1 to Arsenal at Maine Road. City were down 4-0 inside of 20 minutes and the entire stadium decided to turn it into a party. The City faithful cheered on every Arsenal pass and a streaker tried to tackle Kanu, all in front of a brand-new England manager named Sven-Goran Eriksson.

Some more Blues begin to filter in and Joel Buchanan draws a parallel between City with his hometown Texas Rangers baseball club, 'They've never won a championship and they wear blue,' he says.

'I can relate,' I reply.

The next man through the door is someone who, if you meet even just once, is never going to let you forget his name. Enter Joey McCune.

Joey rolls in brash, loud, and just about as you'd imagine a Texan enters a bar. He's 25, well built, sports the latest footballer-haircut, and from what I can gather fancies himself the funniest man in the room. If my first impression of Joey is an unfavourable one, I'll soon be proven wrong.

After nearly going bankrupt and a flight that almost didn't get to Dallas at all, the match with Blue Moon Dallas finally kicks off and we are 30-plus vocal City supporters to Chelsea's silent five. Liz Inga and her brother Marcus – whom Liz got into City only recently by way of mutual admiration for David Silva – assume their lucky spot at the bar, and The Londoner Pub in Frisco, Texas, the official heart of the city and home of Manchester City's official supporters club is ready for a showdown. It's pistols at high noon here in the Wild West.

Over near central London, boot touches ball, and here in Dallas, at The Londoner a group of Texan Blues erupts into song, singing that won't stop for the duration of this match, nor well after the final whistle. In this season's journey, Dallas will be rivalled only by 'The Pit' in Toronto and a rowdy bunch in Hong Kong, when it comes to pub singing, two cities I would not have suspected would win such a distinction when my travels began.

Chelsea draws first blood when André Schürrle walks in a cross from his striker. It's the first peep we hear from the Chelsea quintet sitting at the back, and it isn't exactly melodic, more along the lines of deep caveman-esque grunts. The Dallas Blues don't miss a beat, firing back with a chorus of, 'Have you been, have you been, have you been to Stamford Bridge?' It is a slightly ironic chant as half the Blues in the pub have yet to visit Manchester for a match, but I have little doubt that will change in the weeks, months and years to come.

We land at half-time with Chelsea up 1-0. In the first half, which essentially produced nothing for City to celebrate, Mulvy was easily the loudest in a group of impressively vocal City supporters. During the half he shuffles excitedly from table to table for jittery 30-second conversations concerning which players to bring on for the second half. As I watch Mark live and die with every word spoken by his pub mates, I can't help but wonder, 'Jesus if Mark gets this excited just talking about City, what is he like when they actually score a goal?'

Just minutes after the restart, I witness an event that will be burned into my memory for life. In the 48th minute, Sergio Aguero hits what will easily go down as one of City's top five strikes of the year. A one-time belter from the left edge of the box, short-side past a stunned Petr Cech. And now I have my answer to what happens when the coiled spring that is Mark Mulvanny finally sees a goal.

The best I can describe Mulvy's celebration is a shirtless Tasmanian devil, having just downed a bottle of uppers. Mark tears shirt from body and helicopters it around his head a few times before firing it at The Londoner's giant pull-down theatre screen. Next the half-naked father of two – who are both in attendance – completes a full lap of the pub all the while shouting, 'Are you fucking kidding me!' over and over and, yep, there he is rubbing it in at the Chelsea table, and over again.

There are, it should be pointed out, still families, neutral families, Christian families, in the pub simply trying to enjoy their Sunday brunch. Mark's celebration in the heart of Texas and the shocked reaction of its non-City patrons is worth every penny invested in this journey so far.

The next 40-odd minutes on the pitch are extremely intense as the two early favourites for the championship battle it out. Texan Blues bite their nails, sing, anything to release some of the palpable tension. Everyone except one Blue that is; Virgil Werley appears to be in a dream, easily the happiest and most relaxed person in the room. As he speaks with a fellow Blue a few tables away from me, I eavesdrop, such is my chosen line of work this year. What I overhear is a man telling another man not about football, or American football, or trucks, or guns, or politics, or barbecue. What I overhear is a man speaking endlessly and glowingly about his 13-month-old daughter, Allie, and how she has him completely wrapped around her little finger.

By the 90th minute all signs are pointing towards a 1-1 draw away at the Bridge, and it's a point we'll gladly take, confident in the fact that the Blues will murder Chelsea when we face them back at the Etihad.

Mere minutes from the referee's final whistle, disaster strikes when Matija Nastasic and Joe Hart team up for a calamitous error. The young Serbian defender attempts to routinely head the ball safely back to his keeper in the final minute of the match, without realizing Hart has inexplicably come out to challenge. When the ball arrives at City's goalmouth the only person there to greet it is Fernando Torres. And if you are a non-football fan reading this book, here's a bit of unfortunate news: Fernando Torres does not play for City.

Just like that, in a flash, the point is lost, and an additional two are granted to our title-contending rivals. In a league often decided by a single point, this misstep could have serious implications further down the road. The Chelsea supporters at the back of the pub, quiet for most of the match, roar, and errrr-ahh, and grunt their primal celebrations, which is hardly surprising given Mulvy's earlier taunting.

The Dallas Blues, in true Manchester City fashion, don't hang their heads for long. A few minutes after the final whistle, a conga line forms featuring a team sheet of Mark Mulvanny, Virgil Werley and Joey McCune and snakes its way around the pub, making sure to swing by the Chelsea table on its route, all the while singing, 'City's going down with a billion in the bank' at full volume. Time for a few post-match beers.

As we wait for our pints of local IPA to arrive, I decide to wander over to the Chelsea table for a chat with the three remaining supporters left celebrating their big win – grumpy tracksuit boyfriend and girlfriend having left for what I will assume is an outlet mall somewhere. The three men, whom I earlier referred to as caveman-esque, are gracious in victory and admit they respect how much singing the City supporters do, win, lose, or draw. We chat for a few minutes and before I return to the sky-blue section of The Londoner, Michael, Chris and another Michael all assure me they have indeed been to Stamford Bridge.

Virgil Werley and Joey McCune, from what I can gather, are the Dallas Blues' resident drinkers. The three of us saddle up to one of The Londoner's many round tables and the waitress arrives with four 5oz glasses, each with a different local beer, expertly selected by Virgil. I take a sip of each and decide 4 Corners Local Buzz is the one for today, and in fact, this wins my award for best beer I'll have this season.

Virgil asks if I'm going to finish the other samplers and when I tell him I'm fine, he quickly downs the 15 leftover ounces. If I think this might be a sign of a drinking session between me, Joey and Virgil, I am surprisingly mistaken. Virgil brings me back a full pint of 4 Corners and tells us all he is going home.

You can learn a lot from asking someone to stay a little longer. And when I ask Virgil to stay for another drink I learn he, just like Mo and Anthony Youngblood back in DC, was in the US Military – a firefighter in the Air Force, with the rank of Senior Airman, E-4. While stationed in Japan, Virgil met his wife, Ayako, the two eventually moving to Texas, having their daughter and joining Virgil's son Kade. I learn that the baby took ill almost immediately after her birth and that their best and only affordable healthcare option was for Ayako to return to Japan with newborn Allie.

'They were away for more than a year, and it was almost too much to bear,' Virgil says.

He studies the Blues still at the bar: Mulvy, Joey, Joel.

'These people here, this club, this is the only thing that got me through; I love coming here, I'll always love coming here. But apart from that all I want is to be around Ayako, Allie and Kade.'

I asked Virgil to stay for a drink and couldn't have imagined a better 'no thank you'.

There is another Blue missing in Frisco today. His name is Todd Oliver and his story speaks perfectly to the welcoming nature of Manchester City supporters. At the beginning of last season, Todd decided he wanted to start following English football. His first step would be choosing a side. Todd decided he would watch a match at every supporters club he could find in Dallas and based on the atmosphere of each, choose his allegiance. Chelsea told him to fuck off, Tottenham told him to fuck off, and Newcastle asked if he would be willing to take on the chairman's duties. Love them Geordies.

The final and most welcoming group on Todd's quest for a club was the group I am sitting with today. Again, as I say, you only ever need an introduction to City. Enjoy the drug, Todd.

If you close your eyes and imagine what a Texas police officer in his early 50s looks like, you are likely picturing Tom Haney: rugged square jaw, giant hands, and a spotlessly barbered grey crew cut, which hasn't lost a single hair in its lifetime. Tom has simply moseyed by on his way out the door, to shake my hand, say hello, and with that great Texan sense of hospitality, thank me for coming. But funny things can happen when you ask someone to stay a little longer. I ask Tom to sit down for a few minutes, let me pick his brain, just a few questions.

Tom's voice is deep, not loud, just deep. His words are measured and carefully chosen and he says things like 'I'm gonna be honest with ya buddy' and 'fixin' to'. Tom tells me of growing up a military brat, his father, a master sergeant in the US Air Force, was stationed in Italy – the place Tom first fell in love with soccer. Tom and I both love soccer and we both love Manchester City. Apart from that, Tom Haney and I agree on absolutely nothing.

Tom is what you might refer to as right-wing, whereas I am very much left-wing – and left-wing Canadian at that. Tom believes in privatized healthcare: I believe in socialized medicine. Tom isn't too into the idea of gun control and clings tightly to their Second Amendment, whereas I don't see the point in owning firearms. I tell Tom I am in favour of ending marijuana prohibition, and Tom flashes me his badge.

It's fascinating sitting down with someone so diametrically opposed to my beliefs, all the while the conversation never coming anything close to heated. When I challenge Tom on his fiercely held beliefs, he doesn't snap, or yell at me, handcuff me or drive me to the city limits. There is no animosity towards me, even though I openly disagree with most of what he is saying. Instead, the two of us calmly continue our conversation for 90 more minutes, Tom telling me why he believes what he does and never disrespecting the fact I believe what I do.

It is exactly the way discourse should be. It is, as my grandfather taught me, 'The way we come to understand one another.'

What struck me about Tom was he wasn't some yahoo on Fox News, spouting vitriol and shouting down his opponent, and I like to think what impressed Tom about me was my genuine interest in how he arrived at his views while still standing up for mine. We spend nearly two hours agreeing on almost nothing, and having a superb time doing so.

And how did Tom become a City supporter? A few years back his eldest son, Thomas, while away on an exchange programme in England, mailed his younger brother, Alex, a Shaun Wright-Phillips jersey. From there the City fever spread through the Haney household, just as it did at the Websters'. Perhaps we do have something in common after all.

I come away from our nearly two-hour chat with the impression of Tom as a man who loves his family, loves his state and loves his city; a man you could count on in a pinch. Months from now, in this very spot, Tom will come to Mulvy's aid when Mark bites off more than he can chew in a bar fight. A drunken Dallas Cowboys fan will insult Jules, and in trying to defend his wife's honour Mark will receive a vicious head-butt straight to the nose. When Mark comes to, he will find Tom Haney holding the large offender in a crunching headlock and calmly whispering into the bully's ear, 'I'm a cop.'

Don't mess with Texan Blues.

As afternoon approaches, a new crowd begins funnelling into The Londoner, here to watch their beloved Dallas Cowboys play the Detroit Lions. The remaining Blues are Mark and Joey McCune. Joey, whose first impression left me thinking comedian, or frat boy, Joey who tells me he got into Manchester City in 1999 when he was 11 years old, after ESPN showed highlights of some miracle comeback in some English soccer play-off that completely captured his imagination. Joey has been a City supporter longer than I have.

The more I speak with Joey one-on-one, the more I realize how wrong my first impression was, his constant talking now so obviously enthusiasm versus any kind of arrogance. Joey absolutely consumes Manchester City; he is an encyclopedia when it comes to the boys in blue. He, as much as anyone I will meet, has researched City's history, respects the club's supporters, their songs, their traditions, the local pubs, hell, he even respects their lowly bloggers.

Could it be my first impression was prejudiced because Joey is a good ten years younger than I am? Could it be I'm reaching an age where I'm instantly jealous of youth? Perhaps it was simply because his haircut is cooler and he is in better shape than I am, which caused me to judge him negatively. Joey is not arrogant, he is not a frat boy, and he is not a know-it-all. Joey is kind, he is giving, and he is an expert listener. Joey McCune is a Texan and its time we got him to the Etihad.

Dallas, Texas

Mark and I stroll through a local sporting goods store. I want to see if I can find an FC Dallas top as a souvenir, but I think both of us are taken aback when we discover City tops in the heart of Texas. I hold the home kit in front of Mark:

'Ever think you'd see the day?'

'Never, mate.'

It's finally time for some barbecue. With the kids back home with Jules, Mark and I jump in his Honda and tear off down the highway. During the ride I find out Mark and his family are practising vegetarians, but he assures me my request for a lunch of flame-broiled animals is fine by him.

'Don't worry, mate, a few weeks ago Domino's "accidentally" put pepperoni on the family pizza and I was "forced" to eat it all myself,' he confesses.

'So you'll have some barbecue with me then?'

'Yeah, go on. Just don't let Jules and the kids know.'

The Bishop Arts District is a gentrified, and I suppose for lack of a better word 'hipster' area of Dallas, though I dislike such distinctions. Within the Bishop Arts District exists a smokehouse, and not just any smokehouse. In my life's history this will become *the* smokehouse. Lockhart Smokehouse.

Lockhart Smokehouse, Lockhart Smokehouse, Lockhart Smokehouse. I could write this name over and over again – and grow more ravenous by the keystroke. There is good food, there is great food, and then there is food you would consider moving your entire life for. I would consider moving to Dallas, to the Bishop Arts District, just to be nearer to Lockhart Smokehouse.

Mark and I order ribs, and pulled pork, and chicken, and sausages and perhaps my favourite thing about Texas, macaroni and smoked beans as our sides. Mark, as he did at The Londoner, pays for everything, even though he has no idea just how broke I am. It won't be the last time a Blue picks up the tab; it won't be the last time I'm broke.

'Would you be up for going to another bar with me and having one more beer?' Mark asks.

'I'm up for as many bars as you want to visit, mate.'

For the next hour we sit at Ten Bells Tavern, a very cool sort of country shack, something of a juke joint you'd imagine in the Deep South. Mark nurses a Corona; I enjoy two or three more local beers – the craft scene in Texas alive and well.

I've been to Dallas twice now, the first time being with my dad to see the Kennedy museum. I loved that trip. This weekend was my second time in Dallas, and I loved it all over again.

A few months from now Austin, Texas, will receive an Official Supporters Club designation, and provide City fans even further impetus to visit the great state of Texas. And who knows, maybe this traditionally red state is fixin' to turn blue.

7
HALF-TIME

Home Without A Rest

AFTER YOU clear customs at Toronto's Pearson International Airport, the final barrier separating you from your eagerly awaiting loved ones is a simple set of sliding doors. For as long as I can remember, the person on the other side of these familiar doors has been my father, Bill Webster. Band tours gone wrong, chasing the girl to Barcelona, a few months spent living in Manchester, another year spent in Los Angeles – my dad has always been the first one here to welcome me back, congratulatory hugs for the successful trips, comforting embraces for the ones that didn't quite work.

I'm not sure why this time feels different, maybe time, age, perspective; perhaps it is the fresh memory of my former business partner Reilly having just lost his father; but for whatever reason I allow myself the terrible thought that there will almost certainly come a day when I arrive at Pearson International Airport, these familiar frosted doors will swing open and my dad will no longer be the one there to greet me.

The day someone else collects me from Pearson will be a difficult day, but today is not that day. Today, the frosted doors slide open releasing hundreds of weary travellers, and my dad is standing front and centre, wearing a UCLA hat and signature moustache I've never known him without. His wide smile and sweeping wave cut through the large crowd, and he doesn't appear the least bit annoyed that his 36-year-old son, only days earlier, needed an emergency $200 loan.

'Your mother has sandwiches and a water in the car for you,' he tells me after a welcome-home hug.

On 1 November, Reilly and I throw open the doors on a joint venture in Newmarket, Ontario, the town right next to where I grew up. The Man Cave is a sports-themed seasonal shop that complements the existing shop we used to own together. Time to put my head down and get to work. If we do this right, I'll have enough money to tackle the world in the new year.

I take two and a half days off between 1 November and 30 December. On the half-day, my dad and I watch City throttle Tottenham. Just before the half-time whistle, with City up 1-0, I decide to run to the shop for eggs. By the time I'm back it's 5-0 and when the final whistle blows, City have their largest margin of victory ever, versus Spurs; City 6, Tottenham 0. And it's a result that comes only a few weeks after City's astonishing 7-0 destruction of Norwich.

During my break from the road, City go on an unprecedented tear of 13-1-1 in all competitions, outscoring their opponents 50-17. By contrast, my record when visiting supporter pubs to date is a much less encouraging three wins, two defeats and one draw. Not terrible, but I am starting to entertain the idea that my presence at away supporter clubs is perhaps some sort of jinx.

My second day off comes on 7 December, and it isn't because City play Southampton, it is, rather, a day off because of the night before. Victoria, Mark Zanatta, and Andrew Tripp, my friends from MCFC Chicago, made the nine-hour drive to Toronto to join me at Opera Bob's for the weekend.

On the Friday night, the travelling Chicago Blues arrive with a bottle of Malört, and despite my best efforts to avoid this poison in Chicago, everyone at Bob's will fall victim to Malört's sorcery on the evening of 6 December. For me, I would say Malört tastes like a mixture of paint thinner and soiled linen. But I think bartender Marina describes it best, 30 seconds after her first shot causes her upper lip to curl into her left ear:

'God, it just keeps getting worse!'

So 7 December is my first full day off in 36 days, MCFC Chicago once again doing their worst to me. I manage to catch the first half of the match at Opera Bob's before making the painful 45-minute journey up to the shop. When I finally crawl in around 1pm, Reilly takes one look at my Malört-addled face, decides it will scare children, and mercifully sends me home.

My second and final full day off is spent in Newmarket. Jason Beckford, former City forward, has recently moved his family here from Manchester to accept the technical director's position with Newmarket Soccer Club. Jason's best mate is City legend Paul Lake, and Paul is close with our chairman Dan Reynolds, the two famously marching the Premier League trophy into Opera Bob's last year. Lakey put Jason in touch with Dan, and Danny, knowing I would be in Newmarket for two months, quickly reached out to me and Woody, who had just bought his first Canadian home here.

Our night out comes just a week after the Chicago Blues leave town, and with the taste of Malört still firmly pasted to the roof of my mouth, I want nothing to do with drink. Instead I offer to chaperone Beckford, Danny and Woody to various bars in town. Danny, with an expensive taste for tequila, racks up a bill so dear, I think Woody entertained pulling a runner.

Beckford and Danny are well up to the task when it comes to a night on the piss, and I think Jason seemed genuinely happy to be out with a few Blues in his new town. Two-Bud Wood, however, needs to be poured back into my car by the end of the night. Woody took one for the team and I know had I tried keeping up with Danny and Beckford, I'd have been in a similar state. Still, the sight of Dan Reynolds and a man who has scored for Manchester City carrying Woody across a busy street like a game of Frogger isn't an image I'll soon forget.

On 30 December we close the doors on our temporary store, once again rendering me unemployed. Early in the new year, Jess and I drive up to Montreal, where by the end of the season there will be another new Manchester City OSC. We collect Jess's things from her apartment in Notre Dame de Grâce and make the five-hour journey back to Toronto in ten, thanks to an epic Canadian blizzard. Jess has finished uni and we decide it's time to take a chance on her moving in with me – just as I am getting ready to leave again. That is of course, if I get to leave at all. Two major obstacles now stand in my way, one of them known to me, the other, a hurdle I hadn't counted on.

The first impediment is, of course, the same one 99 per cent of us battle every day – money.

Momentum behind the book is gaining, but there are still no sponsors in terms of flights and I didn't make the sort of money I thought I would over Christmas, nowhere near it in fact. I apply for more credit and cross my fingers. The shop may not have made me rich, but over the past two years it has at least left me with a decent credit rating (which will soon be obliterated). At the last minute, I am approved for a second credit card.

I buy a one-way flight to Manchester for 2 February and a match ticket for 3 February. I'll stay at my sister's place and plan the next moves from over there. I know I desperately want to see Hong Kong; I was researching it a bit in the lead-up to this project and I can't seem to get it out of my mind. And the United Arab Emirates. Given our club's ownership, Abu Dhabi feels like a must visit. The trip is back on. Or so I believe.

Half-time

So here we are, Saturday 1 February, the night before I fly out to Manchester. I still have no clue where I'll go past that, and as I lay awake beside a peacefully sleeping Jess, I run through the different possibilities: Brisbane, Oslo, Abu Dhabi, Hong Kong; something about Hong Kong still bothers me. I read something online about it a few months back, something I was supposed to remember. Oh well, no sense staying up all night worrying, I'll figure it out tomorrow when I finally get back to Manchester.

At 7am I awake with a jolt. It's that scene from every movie in which a sleeping protagonist is awoken with an exaggerated sit-up-quickly-and-gasp by some chilling realization.

'Shit!' I yell, leaping out of bed in the same breath.

In that strange moment right before asleep becomes awake, it came back to me. Hong Kong. Hong Kong, I had read somewhere on the internet, requires six months validity remaining on your passport before entering. And if Hong Kong has that rule, which other countries demand the same? Surely not Britain, please don't tell me Britain. I scramble to find my passport, 'No, no, no,' I murmur as I dig though the drawer where it has sat idle since returning from Dallas. 'Three months you had to look into this, *three* months you idiot!'

I find my passport and almost can't bear to peel back the cover and reveal page three. One deep breath, 'Come on, please don't do this.'

Valid through: July 5, 2014

I quickly deploy the fingers on my left hand and count off the months, desperately hoping my right will be needed next, 'February, March, April, May, June, FUCK!'

With a budget literally down to the penny, a flight that leaves in hours and a match ticket already booked, what choices do I have? I could cancel the flight, stay here another week and rush a new passport through. But between the passport rush and cost of switching the flight, that would set me back another $400 before I've even started. And with a budget down to the penny, $400 would certainly mean crossing another city off my list, not to mention I have a ticket for City versus Chelsea tomorrow where I'm supposed to meet up with Dan Reynolds and Ross's dad, Bobby. My only chance is to get on this plane, cross my fingers Britain doesn't require the six-month validity nonsense and figure this mess out from England.

So here we go, with a one-way ticket and a potentially dodgy passport. Not sure the UK Border Agency – or anywhere else for that matter – will let me in, but leaving feels like my only move. Time to go knock on a few doors and see what happens.

SECOND HALF

SECOND HALF

8
MANCHESTER

Blue Tuesday

I LOVE flying into Manchester. Bursting through thick stratus clouds into a world of lush greens surrounded by Victorian brick and the turbine-dotted Pennines. For me heaven exists just below this soft grey duvet over East Manchester.

Good old Blighty; the Brits like to employ something called common sense when it comes to the issue of passport validity. So long as your passport is valid for the entirety of your intended visit, you're all good. So we're in, and in many ways, back to where it all began.

Tell me where else in the world you could walk into a chain-grocer and hear the Stone Roses over the PA, immediately followed by Bob Dylan's 'Blowin' in the Wind'? Football allegiances aside, I have fallen in love with Manchester as a whole. I love the way it always welcomes me back with open arms, a tall pint, and a tuna crunch from Greggs. I love the way it looks out for my little sister when her big brother can't be here. I love the record shops for still knowing who The Charlatans are and stocking The Inspiral Carpets on vinyl. I love The Brook Pub on a Sunday and a curry take-away from The Mahbub in Chorlton.

Danny Reynolds and I meet at Sinclair's Oyster bar in the heart of Manchester. If you have been to or seen one pub in Manchester it is likely Sinclair's, its three-story black-and-white tudor-trim exterior is a major landmark in these parts. Meeting us here this evening is Wythenshawe-born Bobby Simnor, the man who moved to Campbell River British Columbia in the 1970s to start a family with a Canadian woman he'd chased halfway around Greece. When they finally settled on the western shores of Canada they had two children: Rob and Ross, the latter eventually moving to Toronto and opening a pub that would change the direction of my life.

I can't recall if I shared this fact with Bobby or not, such was my exhaustion and I left my notebook back at the flat, in favour of a match ticket, no sense messing around with handwritten notes on my first night of jet lag. In fact, perhaps this is a good time to take a moment and provide a few hard-earned tips I've learned over years of flying into Manchester. To my North American brothers and sisters still planning their first visit here, make note. When you take the overnight flight from North America – which you should do because it is by far the most affordable option – three options will present themselves.

1. Sleep On The Plane: The most pragmatic plan that comes to mind is always, 'I'll board at 11pm, be asleep by midnight, sleep seven hours and wake up in Manchester.' Good luck with that. The best you'll get on an overnight flight to Manchester is an hour or two nap here or there, and here's how you'll achieve that; one anti-nausea pill and two pints of Guinness. That should fetch you a few hours' shut eye, but you're still going to land at pre-dawn our time, midday local time.

2. Power Through: This is the tactic I would employ in my younger days. Get a few drinks in at the airport, then coffee and movies on the plane, arriving energized at Manchester International Airport. Get back to my sister's flat for early afternoon and start on the beers. Now you're going to try to power through. Keep the party going until around 10 or 11pm, and having been up for around 30 hours at this point, crash hard and wake up at 8am, body clock adjusted. Sounds perfect, right? It is perfect... if you're still in your 20s. If you're a day past 30, 'power through' should be taken off your list of options.

3. The Mélange: Implementing the best parts of the two plans is ultimately going to be your most effective course of action. Arrive at the airport early: it will eliminate a measure of stress. Find a bar serving Guinness; every airport has one and we want consistency here. Drink exactly two pints of Guinness over 45–90 minutes. *Do not* exceed two pints unless you're Irish, in which case you've stopped listening to me ages ago. The moment your plane's wheels leave the tarmac, knock back an anti-nausea pill, making absolutely sure it's of the drowsy variety. Seriously, who are these people who take non-drowsy pills? Such a waste.

This will buy you about two to three hours of interrupted sleep, perhaps uninterrupted, if you've scored a window seat. You're going to land in Manchester dead tired, no way around this fact, but what we're aiming for here is the quickest adjustment possible. If we do this right, you're going to be ready to go and on UK time by tomorrow.

When you arrive at where you'll be staying, power through for another hour or two and then take a 90-minute nap: *do not* exceed 90 minutes. Set your alarm and wake up somewhere between 3 and 5pm. Brew a tea or a coffee to shake the cobwebs off. Next, set off into town for two to three pints of ale or easy-drinking lager: *do not*, under any circumstances, drink Stella. Aim to get back home for around 10pm. Power through for one more hour, and take some form of cold medication around 10.40pm. Head to bed at 11pm and with any luck you'll be up by 10am, ready to attack a magical day in the capital of the North.

Monday 3 February. City v Chelsea. 8pm kick-off

A quick ten-minute ride in a black cab brings us to 13 Grey Mare Lane, and the most famous Man City pub in the world, Mary D's, a two-story, five-room, booze-fuelled Manchester City emporium. The front bar houses a few pool tables and giant pull-down TV screen. The room to the right of the front bar is the size of any regular pub and decorated as such. Walk through towards the back and you're in a lobby of sorts, a small booth selling Manchester City souvenirs in the far corner. Across from this booth is a set of stairs, guarded by a large security guard, causing the upper level to appear somewhat exclusive, or shady, or perhaps both, I can't be sure.

Myself, Dan and Bobby head into the main room at Mary D's, an open-space venue where City supporters are packed shoulder to shoulder, surrounded by decades worth of flags and memorabilia adorning the walls, all set to the sound of a DJ playing Kasabian's 'Club Foot'. It's like a history lesson inside the best party you've ever been to. Oh, and it's Monday night.

Two pints and a few Oasis tunes later, Bobby and I have had enough of shouting over the music, we're starving and the balti pies at the Etihad begin to call our names. Danny has disappeared up the mystery staircase. He needs to go and meet a man named Howard Burr, membership secretary of Manchester City Supporters Club, and tells us to meet him at the match.

A three-minute walk in February's brisk evening air places me and Bobby Simnor on the doorstep of Ashton New Road, home of Manchester City Football Club. The Etihad has only been our ground since 2003, built first for the Commonwealth Games in 2002 with the intention of becoming City's new home afterwards.

My one great regret as a City supporter is that I was too late to the party to visit Maine Road, City's former home. I'm told Maine Road was rundown, lacked modern amenities and was the greatest stadium that ever stood. Our new home is a penthouse suite comparatively, but could a penthouse suite elicit more emotion, more nostalgia than the house you grew up in? Could a one-night stand ever be more memorable than your first kiss? Not a chance. As such, many Blues miss and still yearn for the days of Maine Road.

If the company and the balti pies are spot-on, the match is anything but. Chelsea have our number again, and though it is Ivanovic who strikes the game's lone tally, Eden Hazard is easily the most creative and dangerous man on the pitch tonight. It should have been two before the half, Samuel Eto'o having hit the post. Gary Cahill hit the post in the second half, and this match could easily have ended 3-0 tonight. It's our first loss at home this season, but myself, Danny and Bobby are left thinking what most of the other 40,000 Blues in attendance are: surely this is Chelsea's league to lose.

On the way home, Danny and I duck in to the Mitre Hotel's bar for one final drink. There he tells me that in the morning he will fly to Tel Aviv, and though he doesn't mention it, I suspect our now-former chairman has fallen in love.

Manchester

The following day finds me suffering a mild crisis of confidence as I sit in the lobby of the new BBC buildings in Salford. I'm here to take part in Manchester City's weekly radio programme, hosted by Ian Cheeseman, called *Blue Tuesday*. I've been waiting for nearly 30 minutes and still no one has come to meet me. The receptionist asks me if I have Mr Cheeseman's phone number and I tell her I do not. The best she can offer is to email him and hope he sees it.

I feel foolish sitting here, wearing blue jeans in a lavish new radio and television studio, as good-looking men and women wearing even better-looking clothes stride confidently by, greeting one another with the sort of familiarity one uses when they're somewhere they belong. It all has me feeling like I don't belong. After all, I wasn't born in Manchester. And I didn't even get into soccer until I was 17. So what exactly *am* I doing here? Who could possibly give a shit about what I have to say? And where is Ian Cheeseman already – does anyone even know I'm supposed to be on tonight's show?

Originally it was meant to be Danny Reynolds discussing being the chairman of an overseas supporters club, but he's somewhere over Turkey right now, leaving me here to fill his spot. The BBC didn't even want me here in the first place, so again I have to ask myself, 'What the fuck am I doing here?'

Just as I contemplate a dash towards the exit to grab the nearest tram back to my sister's flat, a man – actually no, man isn't the right word here – a *presence* walks through the revolving doors, wearing a long black coat with slicked-back white hair on a head that easily stands six and a half feet above sea level. I can only see the side of his face, but I feel as though we've met before. The presence strides assertively towards the same receptionist I dealt with about a half-hour previously.

'Joe Corrigan here for Ian Cheeseman,' he says, turning towards the couches before the woman at the desk can even ask if he knows Ian's phone number.

For those of you who don't know, Joe Corrigan was City's number one keeper through the 1970s and into the early '80s. Joe won two League Cups and the European Cup Winners' Cup with City and on nine occasions suited up for England.

Within minutes of Joe's arrival, Tony Prescott, Ian Cheeseman's right-hand man on *Blue Tuesday*, comes rushing into the lobby, greets Joe and asks the two of us to follow him. As we sit in the green room on the third floor of the remarkable new BBC buildings in Media City, prepping for the show, I remind Joe that we met briefly once before.

'You came and spoke at our supporters club in Toronto, two seasons ago.'

'Of course, I love Toronto! We had a great night there,' Joe replies. 'So what are you doing over here?'

I nervously tell Joe about my book idea, and before he can offer his thoughts, Tony returns and grabs his attention, 'Joe, we just need you to do a bit of pre-roll for tonight's show.'

Joe excuses himself and heads for the booth. I sip the last bit of my tea and go back to wondering what the hell I'm doing here. When Joe returns from the booth, it's just the two of us sitting across from each other, minutes before the show.

'You know, I've been thinking more about your idea. I think it's absolutely brilliant what you're doing. Have you been to Oslo yet?' he asks.

It's all the encouragement I need to keep going, and when I overhear Joe a few minutes later telling Tony, 'Have you heard what that Canadian lad is doing? Isn't it brilliant?' I'm left positively buzzing, all insecurities gone thanks to a few motivational breaths from a proper City legend.

Myself, Ian Cheeseman, Tony Prescott, the engaging and hilarious Kuczaj brothers, Mark and Joe, along with producer Neda Druzic, and big Joe Corrigan lay down a belting hour of live radio. With a fierce wind at my back it's time to decide my next move, because when big Joe Corrigan tells you you're doing something well, you bloody well keep doing it.

After doing *Blue Tuesday*, I receive an invitation to the Etihad Stadium for the monthly general meeting of the Official Manchester City Supporters Clubs, which covers a wide range of topics from matchday parking to Christmas parties, and most interestingly to me, which cities get granted official supporter clubs.

During my visit, Vancouver and Gibraltar are announced as the newest member branches, bringing the global total to 154. Howard Burr, the man Danny met at Mary D's, invites me to say a few words. The morning after the meeting, the chairman of the entire committee,

Kevin Parker, sends out an email to all 154 chairpersons, explaining to them what I'd said the night previous.

Within 48 hours I receive more emails than I could possibly respond to and I'm up until 2am just to get through half. Howard and Kevin create more interest in one email than I have been able to drum up in six months. I'm off to the races and the invitations start coming fast and furious.

I've been able to do some research regarding my passport issue. It looks like I was wrong on Hong Kong, they only require one month validity and remain very much in the running. Anywhere in Europe is three months, under something known as the Schengen agreement. I'm hearing conflicting information on Abu Dhabi, some sources say 90 days, others six months, but we'll cross that bridge when and if it ever comes. For now I have invites from some pretty enticing destinations: everywhere from Malta to Cape Town, Costa Blanca to Sierra Leone. There are also some lesser-known places in my inbox such as Jersey, Dukinfield and Donegal.

And then there's this invite from a gang calling themselves the Wight Blues, who meet in Cowes on the Isle of Wight. Just where is this Isle of Wight? It has a certain ring to it. As I sit in front of my computer in my sister's living room, the lonely lights of Strangeways prison flickering from across the road, I say the name a few times out loud, 'The Isle of *Wight*. The *Isle* of Wight. It sounds exotic, yet innocent. And it isn't too far from Manchester. Yeah, the Isle of Wight, this sounds like a good place to ease my way back on to the road.

9

ISLE OF WIGHT

I'm Going Robbed?

I COME to around 5.30am feeling like Aleksandar Kolarov just belted a free kick directly into my face. I gently roll myself off the bed, barely making it to my feet. Why is my shoulder killing me? The drapes were left open and an early grey sunlight, a painful sunlight, pours into the small and oddly shaped corner room.

What the hell happened? I haven't blacked out much in my life, and it's been quite a while since the last time, but for some reason, on the rare occasions I do, one of my immediate thoughts is always, 'How much money did I spend?'

I'm on a shoestring budget here and I know how careless I can be with money when I'm drinking. I stagger towards my jacket, which lies in a crumpled heap on the floor. *Holy shit*, bending down to pick the jacket up was an awful idea; my head nearly bursts like a water balloon filled too tightly. I rummage through my coat pockets and come up with exactly nothing; where the hell is my cash? Jeans perhaps? Yeah that's it, must be in my jeans. But where the hell are my jeans? Okay, there they are over by the… Holy shit what happened to that desk? It looks like someone picked up a full curry take-away and in some inexplicable disagreement with an innocent desk shouted, 'Fuck you desk!' then – wham! Splat! – a full curry meal to the poor desk's face.

Well, no time to figure out the desk mystery, I gotta find out where all my money went. I turn all four jean-pockets inside out and again come up with nothing. This simply can't be. The Isle of Wight gang was buying me drinks all night; I swear I didn't pay for a thing. So where could all my cash have gone? Okay, let's think this through; I need clues. First obvious place to check is my cellphone. Aha! There are late-night text messages. Let's see, who was the last person I…ah, here we go, I wrote Jess around 2am, this should tell us something; opening up the message and:

Text to Jess: *Babe, I am going robbed, I think it is important you know.*

What the hell, I got robbed? How do I not remember *this*? Is that why my shoulder hurts? I rush the few steps into the small bathroom to check my face. I don't look pretty, but no visible signs of a struggle. Knuckles? Not a scratch. I briefly try and recreate how a mugging that left only your shoulder hurting might take place. Apart from looking like a tweaking meth addict, alone in my hotel room, this amateur re-enactment solves nothing.

I stare at the text message for a few minutes, unable to take my eyes off this horrifying word, 'robbed'. Just then, a new message arrives. But who could be messaging me at 5.30am?

Text from Vic: *Hey, how was the Isle of Wight? We're still here at the Globe, drinking!*

I type back frantically.

Text to Vic: *It was great…until I got fucking robbed! What's worse is I have absolutely no memory of the event.*

From Vic: *Oh my god I am so sorry! Okay, we'll figure this out together. First things first, let's go over everything you remember.*

Isle of Wight

My journey to the Isle of Wight, which began in Manchester and went via London Euston station (the words 'crowded', 'confusion', and 'mayhem' were surely invented here) was slow and tedious due to the extreme flooding in the south of England. The journey was made even more painful by having to share the train car with rehearsing future-rejects of *X-Factor* or *Britain's Got No Talent*. What I could see of the flooding along the way was heartbreaking.

I set off for the Isle of Wight from the port of Southampton, and if that particular port sounds familiar, it should: *The Titanic* left Southampton 102 years ago, on its way to Cork, the Atlantic and infamy. I will be aboard a slightly less luxurious vessel, but one far more advanced than anything a shipbuilder of the early 1900s could have imagined. The Red Funnel Ferry takes you the ten nautical miles from Southampton to Cowes in under 25 minutes at a maximum speed of 40 knots. By contrast, *Titanic's* ill-advised and fatal top speed was 22 knots.

The Red Funnel Ferry's 'Red Ensign' – which incidentally is the name of Canada's first flag – is a passenger only hydrofoil and what 12-year-old me would have called 'awesome!' Almost hovering over the choppy water at 45mph, it easily feels like 200mph on land, all the while droplets, couplets and entire waves full of English Channel smack against the side of our aquatic rocket ship.

I arrive at the port of Cowes, on the northernmost tip of the Isle of Wight, with about ten minutes to spare before I am to meet my Wight Blue's liaison, so the Fountain Hotel's location, quite literally 20 steps from the dock, is a welcome convenience. I check into my room and take a quick survey of where I'll be sleeping. It's an oddly shaped room, tiny, but quite cosy. The decor is striking, in particular an antique desk that acts as a sort of centrepiece just below a large window. I think to myself, 'I must make use of a desk such as this, perhaps I'll wake up early tomorrow morning and get some writing in before breakfast. Yes, yes I must do this!'

I quickly change my shirt, throw on a coat, as it is a bit chilly here on the island, and head down to the lobby bar where I am to meet John Nightingale – yes, John Nightingale is his real name, and yes, it will be the coolest name to appear in this book.

On my journey thus far, there have been a series of strange first-date type scenarios in which – with the exception of Victoria in Chicago – I arrive in a city and wait for a strange older man to come and meet me. After about 20 minutes of awkwardly giving three or four local Cowes men 'the eye' I notice two tall, City-scarf-clad gentlemen duck their heads into the tiny hotel pub.

'Darryl, John is running late, he's outside trying to find a cash-point. I'm Kev,' the man says.

Kevin Allen looks like a younger, slimmer and clean-shaven Santa Claus. With Kev is Andy Buxton, an equally jovial-looking gentleman, whose bushy white moustache perfectly complements the classic Mancini scarf resting effortlessly around his neck.

If I'm worried we'll be a few minutes late to the Horseshoe pub where the Wight Blues assemble, I needn't be – Andy owns a British racing-green Jaguar. After we collect John from outside the hotel, we climb in with Andy and he tears through the tiny island roads as though he were Damon Hill. Within five minutes, we're where we need to be, with time to spare.

Saturday 15 February. FA Cup Fifth Round. City v Chelsea. 5.15pm kick-off

The tiny Horseshoe Inn at 353 Newport Road, on the tiny 380-square-kilometre Isle of Wight, is like something out of a fairytale; granted it's a grown-man-who-loves-football-pubs-and-ale-drinking's fairytale, but it's a fairytale nevertheless. The Horseshoe is exactly the sort of place I could retire to and as I am greeted by friendly after friendlier local, I briefly contemplate a life here; a sort of utopian existence wherein my only responsibility would be lifting impeccably pulled pints and producing the odd amusing anecdote.

There's a strange murmur travelling around the room in the moments leading up to kick-off. The announcement of an unusual starting 11, which includes Pantilimon, Lescott, Milner, Garcia and Jovetic, has the locals restless. My view is, we've already lost twice to Chelsea this year, why not shake things up a little. These are the sorts of decisions that will show us what our new Chilean manager is made of. For those unfamiliar with the FA Cup, tonight's match is part of a one-and-done knockout-style tournament open to all pro clubs in England. It is the oldest trophy in football and remains a very prestigious award, and is, if I'm being honest, my favourite of all competitions.

I was in Dallas when we lost 2-1 to Chelsea, and at the Etihad just two weeks ago for a heartbreaking 1-0 league defeat. This brings my record to an underwhelming three wins, three defeats and one draw. I am starting to feel like a jinx and confess to John my poor track record. John Nightingale is in his early 50s but you wouldn't know it to look at him. He's in excellent shape, has the sort of fierce hairline that will outlast a nuclear winter, and unique brand of smile that wins elections in a landslide. As a third-generation Blue, his son and daughter now fourth-generation Blues, John believes in City jinxes and I don't think I've done much to calm his nerves by disclosing my run of bad luck.

'Maybe you should leave,' he jokes.

The Horseshoe is a roughly 1,000-square-foot pub with low ceilings and a single flatscreen TV hanging on its far wall. To the right are a fire exit and a sign reminding patrons that dogs are 'no longer' allowed inside the pub. On the wall to my left – hanging just over the heads of the three kids I'd put somewhere between 12 and 14 – is a list of English beers currently on tap. The Horseshoe refers to this list as its 'Guest beer list'. Kev offers to buy my first round and asks me what I'd like. I tell him I'd like to sample all four of the guest selections this evening, starting at the top with Fortyniner, which is fittingly 4.9% alcohol by volume.

I spend my first pint taking in the Horseshoe's village atmosphere, its myriad beer coasters tacked to the wall, and the Wight Blues' little mascot donkey they call Wightchester who wears a City top and, when you press his button, plays the club's theme song and dances about wiggling his ears.

Just as I put the final sip down on what was a decent first ale, John arrives with pint number two, a Wadworth

(4.3%), and the loquacious Peter Finch arrives with his first of many, many stories.

Peter is the sort of human being writers dream of meeting. He is older, wiser and full of stories that he tells with an impeccable sense of timing and detail. His fellow Blues may have become a bit used to Peter's storytelling, however, and when they see the two of us chatting at length, one Blue is heard to shout, 'Enjoy writing the Peter Finch chapters,' which gets a raucous and knowing laugh from the 40-plus members tucked into their tiny local.

Peter, with his shaved head and forearm tattoos, could easily pass for mid-40s, but the more you speak with him you realize the truth likely lies ten years north of this number. Pete asks if I need a drink and I tell him I'm okay for the moment, but that over the course of the night I would like to 'run the table' with the four English ales.

'I had a German mate come in here once,' Peter begins. 'He ran the table twice before deciding he didn't like any of them and went back to drinking Foster's for the rest of the evening. Those German lads can drink you know!'

I'm only a few sips into pint number two when Stefan Jovetic buries a goal into the far corner past a helpless Petr Cech. Pellegrini's line-up choices are looking smarter by the minute. The Wight Blues erupt in celebration, Tom Moriarty so much so that when he jumps into the air, his head knocks one of the speakers off one of the Horseshoe's load-bearing pillars.

At half-time I sit down for my first bit of press aside from Manchester City's website and Blue Tuesday. Word of the book has spread a little bit, and Alan Marriott has come to the Horseshoe on behalf of the *Isle of Wight County Press*. It's nice sitting down with another writer, and the more we talk, the more I realize I am learning as much from this interview as Alan.

As he describes the island's multitude of guests and festivals hosted here over the years – Jimi Hendrix, Kings of Leon, Red Hot Chili Peppers, Outkast – I am humbled that he took the time to sit down with an unknown Canadian quasi-travel writer. After our interview and just before the second half kicks off, Alan snaps a picture of John and I, and I can't help but wonder if years from now this might be my *Motor Cycle Diaries* shot: with me as Che and John as my Alberto Granado. Or perhaps I am Alberto and John Nightingale is Che. Yeah, that's it, I would definitely be Alberto; I like the idea of John Nightingale as the Isle of Wight's Che Guevara.

Pint number three, a King John (4.2%) and my favourite pint of the evening, arrives courtesy of Big Andy, just as City's clinching goal arrives courtesy of tonight's super-sub Samir Nasri. The Wight Blues immediately launch into Samir's old Arsenal song. 'Na-na-na-na-na-Nas-a-ri!' rings off the walls, sung loudest by Ian Gerrard sitting at the far corner of the bar. It's the first time I'm hearing Blues adopt the YouTube viral hit from Arsenal Away Boyz, and three pints in on a relatively empty stomach, it has me in stitches.

In the end, Manuel Pellegrini's moves prove genius. Jovetic scores the winner, Lescott is man of the match, and City are on to the quarter-finals of the FA Cup versus Wigan. And though we lost to Wigan in the FA Cup Final last season, we've already dispatched them 5-0 earlier this year in the League Cup. With the Latics coming to the Etihad, our path to the final appears almost certain.

Peter Finch delivers my fourth and final pint (or so I believe), an easy-drinking ale called Sharp's Doom Bar, and at only 4%, a nice way to wrap up the evening (or so I believe). Peter will tell me an endless number of great stories on this evening, some I will recall, others I won't, but the story he tells about Hong Kong, I could never forget.

'So you remember all those volcanoes going off in Iceland a few years ago, the ones that disrupted flights all over the world? Well I was stuck in bloody Hong Kong for a week, couldn't get out. My missus and me had to scramble to find a hotel and figure out how and when we'd get back to England, but to be honest, all I cared about was finding somewhere to watch the derby. I ended up at some standard sports pub in Kowloon, and it was absolutely packed full of Reds. All except for one poor local lad, who saw me in my City top, came up to me and whispered, "I'm City, too."

'"Don't hide it!" I told him. "And don't worry about these Reds, you're with me!" We spent the rest of the match drinking shots of sambuca together and were the loudest two in the pub.

'Afterwards I invited him to come to England, but unfortunately he and his wife had already booked their holidays to Las Vegas.'

Peter downs the last of his pint and holds up his finger, 'But! Once we finally got back to England, there was a message waiting from my new friend, Marc Luk. "Peter, it's not Sin City, it's Man City! We're coming to see you in England."'

'I'm going to be in Hong Kong this weekend, Marc Luk is my host!' I tell Peter excitedly.

'Well, then let's do some sambuca shots in Marc Luk's honour!' he replies.

Let's do some sambuca shots. I think that's how it went. From here on out things get a little patchy. I absolutely recall having a fantastic chat with Peter's grandson Flynn. Flynn is 13 years old and more mature than Peter and myself put together. His granddad is looking after him for the weekend, but it's more than likely going to end up the other way around, the way this evening is headed.

I shake some more hands, do some more shots and meet a bunch more Wight Blues: John's son Darren, his daughter Laura, Kev's wife Ness, head bartender Claudia Le Moigne and scores of other beautiful souls. But again, this is where it begins to get hazy and my notes are absolutely no help, my penmanship – suspect on my soberest of days – virtually illegible cave etchings by this point in the evening.

The last conversation I have at the Horseshoe is with Pavel Juricek, an ice hockey-mad Slovakian who, like myself, is completely caught up in the Olympic hockey now well underway in Sochi.

I would love to tell you exactly where in Slovakia Pavel is from, exactly when and why he came to the Isle of Wight, and most importantly, how Pavel became a Blue. But sambuca is happening and wiping out memories as quickly as they're created. Come to think of it, why is this sambuca dark? What are we drinking now, Peter? Pavel tutors me in the correct ways of pronouncing famous Slovak players such as Zedeno Chara (Zeh-d-ehno, HAR-ah) while Celine Dion's *Titanic* music video plays on the big screen in the background, an odd Southampton-French Canadian connection even in the soberest of lights; drunk, this is nothing short of mind-blowing.

Seven of us relegate the Horseshoe to the lower division of our evening and sway our way to the next pub, down the narrow streets of Cowes – which I want to say are cobblestone, but hell, who knows? I do know I enjoy a great chat with Mark Anderson, I just can't for the life of me remember what it was about. One thing is for damn sure, I do recall Mark is easy to talk to and how much I enjoyed his company, if not the specifics of our chat.

I'd like to return to Cowes someday and pick up our conversation where I don't remember it leaving off.

Mark and I stumble into what I'm going to call 'Random Downtown Pub', joined by Pavel, Kev, John, Justin Ferdyn and Ness, the designated driver and videographer – yes, video of this evening exists. We are singing 'Blue Moon' and we are a complete mess.

After what I'm assuming was a few pints at Random Pub, we head to a pub I'm going to name 'Pub Three'. This much I know of Pub Three: I met an Arsenal fan who refused to believe I was travelling for a book about City, John fell off a couch, and I committed the single biggest sin any musician can ever commit against a fellow player: stage invasion – first on piano, then on what I believed to be virtuoso backing vocals. If the wildly talented, heroically patient Isle of Wight chap playing Morrissey on his acoustic guitar is by any chance reading this, or any Wight Blues know of whom I speak, then please, from the bottom of my eternally apologetic heart, tell him I am deadly sorry and horrifyingly aware of what an ass clown I am.

I don't exactly remember saying goodbye or leaving Pub Three, but I do know for certain I went for a curry take-away, where I ran into John's daughter Laura and her boyfriend. I remember getting back to The Fountain Hotel and noting that the bar was still open, then telling myself, 'Go upstairs and eat your curry first, then if you still feel up for a drink you can go back down.' Sounds an oddly lucid and rational thought for someone who was presumably just robbed.

Isle of Wight

Back in the room the evidence suggests I ate about half of my curry before deciding to share the rest with the antique desk. Text from me to Vic: *And that's it, that's everything I remember.*

Text from Vic: *I feel like you couldn't possibly remember all of that, but not remember getting robbed?*

Victoria makes a great point. How could I possibly remember everything *except* being robbed? I need to get in the shower, throw up a little and regroup. Which is precisely what I do. Shockingly the shower fails to cure my hangover, or solve the mystery, however as I emerge back into the room I notice a five-pound note lying at the foot of the bed, rumpled in a manner that makes it look like the Queen's had a stroke.

'Hunh? Well, there's a fiver,' I think to myself. I guess the bastards didn't get all of my money. My next order of business is to see if I can get this once gorgeous antique desk back to the way it looked when I first arrived, 12 hours ago. As I scrape and sift through the discarded Indian food I come across about £10-worth of coins. So that's £15, and logging into my banking app I can see I only pulled out 60 to begin with. So why would someone rob me for £45 and not the remaining 15?

And hang on a minute; I must have paid for this curry take-away, that's an easy £10 right there. And come to think of it, I bought a drink for that Arsenal supporter who didn't – nor should he – believe I was any sort of proper writer. Why I'd buy him a drink I'm not sure, but it comes back to me that I did. And I think I bought a round at Random Downtown Pub, and there were six of us there. Have I been robbed at all? Why does my phone say robbed?

I decide to try recreating the text. '*Babe, I'm going robbed, I think it's important you know,*' but in the manner drunk me would type, missing each letter and hitting the letter directly to its left. When you do this (did you just try it?) you quickly notice it is impossible for *getting* to autocorrect to *going*. However, if you were to type 'to bed' and miss the space bar, what would you get? Exactly.

And just to top it off, there was one last text to Jess I hadn't noticed, a message after '*I think it's important you know.*'

Text from me: *I love you*

In the end, I wasn't robbed at all, I simply got hammered drunk on pints and sambuca – and probably some Jäger – and tried to text my girlfriend back home, 'Babe, I'm going *to bed*, I think it's important you know, I love you.'

Isle of Wight will forever be my most debauched chapter, and as a writer, I suppose the most unprofessional. But the Isle of Wight will also be one of my unquestionable favourites, and of all the places I hope to return to, this is one place I know I will. Now if you'll excuse me, I need very badly to go back to bed; Isle of Wight, I think it's important you know: I love you.

10
HONG KONG

Focus

I AM not the sort who cries during a Coen brothers film. So as I fight back tears, midway through *Inside Llewyn Davis* on a KLM flight from Amsterdam to Hong Kong, I am all too aware something is off. Perhaps the scene in which an aspiring musician who, after using the last of his money to get from New York to Chicago, is told by the promoter, 'I don't see a lot of money here,' hits a little too close to home.

But if I'm being completely honest, this sadness has been brewing for a few days now. On Sunday, when I returned from the Isle of Wight, I assumed it was simply the hang-over causing me to feel down. But Monday was worse, and Tuesday worse still. I fear this could be something more.

How is it that I am 'living a dream' as Jess keeps telling me, yet sitting here on the verge of tears, en route to a place I've always dreamed of visiting?

When I first began plotting this book, Hong Kong was a city near, if not tops on my list. I desperately wanted to go, but getting to the South China Sea was always going to eat up a massive part of the budget, and I knew travelling there would likely eliminate Brisbane, and perhaps even Oslo.

In the end two people convinced me to go to Hong Kong – my childhood friend Mark Van De Ven and, of course, Norman – both adamant I write the book, both believing strongly Hong Kong would provide an exotic setting and important contrast to previous cities. So I went. Passport validity isn't going to be a problem here after all, the rule having changed long ago from six months to a much more reasonable one month. Still, as I board my 747 in Amsterdam, the KLM stewardess issues me an ominous heads-up, 'You know, this passport expires soon, you should get it renewed right away.'

The airport in Hong Kong is located on the island of Chek Lap Kok, a swathe of reclaimed land, necessary due to Hong Kong's limited supply of flatlands. I will be staying on Hong Kong Island and I think the hotel offers an airport shuttle to get there, but I've been awake and travelling for nearly 24 hours now; Manchester's Piccadilly station feels like ages ago.

I'm too exhausted to navigate one of the world's largest passenger terminals and look for a shuttle I may or may not have access to. I'm told red cabs are for Hong Kong Island, and when I see a waiting line of red, I approach. The back door opens on it's own, a bizarre pulley system operated by the driver, essentially a rope attaching a handle near his gearbox to the back door. I jump in and pray it comes in under 50 pounds. The cabbie tells me the ride will take us about 45 minutes in morning traffic and cost around 400 Hong Kong dollars, or the equivalent of £30. I can handle this for now; just get me to a bed.

As we draw nearer to the city, the incredible population density of Hong Kong begins to reveal itself. The apartment buildings are like nothing I have ever seen before. The population of the town I grew up in could easily live inside just one of these super-structures, which stretch for miles, one after the other. With the highest concentration of skyscrapers anywhere in the world, you can't be depressed, or sad, or scared, or anything other than completely awestruck when viewing Hong Kong for your first time.

'What is the population of Hong Kong?' I ask the cabbie.

'Uh, I think, uh, 100 years?' he replies.

I attempt to rephrase the question, this time in the truly patronizing style of travelling Westerner, by slowing it down and making the words more phonetic, as if he were to do the same, I might suddenly understand Cantonese.

'Oh no, sorry, I mean how many pee-pull live here? One million? Twen-tee million?'

'Ohhhh, yes, yes, I know!' Finally he understands me. 'Yes, I think is definitely 100 years.'

Hong Kong has 7.5 million inhabitants but you would swear the number is many times that. At only 426 square miles, the Special Administrative Region of the People's Republic of China packs its almost 300 skyscrapers and 7.5 million people into a place the size of Greater Manchester.

Forty-five minutes after leaving the airport, I arrive at the Cosmo Hotel in the Wan Chai district of Hong Kong. I'm too exhausted for sightseeing and have an 11pm kick-off ahead of me. Desperate for a bed, I enter the hotel elevator and punch the button for the 17th floor, and quickly notice floors four and 14 seem to be missing. I'm used to not seeing the 13th floor in North America, but four and 14? What's wrong with four and 14?

Once in my room, I duck into a tiny shower, and then spend the next 20 minutes trying to open the windows in my cramped room, before eventually giving up and finally falling asleep.

I wake at around 8pm, absolutely starving. The last time I woke up was in the Green Quarter of Manchester; I stepped out of my sister's building to a view of Strangeways prison and the Pennines. Stepping out the door to start the following day into a Hong Kong nightscape presents a marked contrast. The sun has long since gone down and my first real sense of Hong Kong comes at night.

After strolling past a park and a few quiet side streets, I arrive at Lockhart Road, in the heart of the Wan Chai district. Wan Chai is one of Hong Kong's top entertainment districts, the layout at the intersection of Luard Road and Lockhart being as follows: restaurant, strip club, British pub, repeat. At 9pm the scene is already somewhere between hedonism and debauchery. I make a right where I should have gone left, and am instantly grabbed at the arm by an elderly woman.

'First one is free,' she cries, desperately trying to drag me into her strip joint. I am unsure whether she means my first drink is free, my first dance is free, or something entirely different. I manage to break free of her death grip and head back the other way.

At about 9.30pm, after stepping into and quickly out of four or five strange restaurants, I settle in for dinner, which for me will be breakfast. Despite a decent rest, I still can't shake this doom and gloom feeling. Alone at my table, five minutes pass, then ten and I can't help but feel like this joint is serving all the locals first. I convince myself it's all in my head, until I see a couple who clearly walked in after me get served, and another couple after them. Maybe I'm supposed to call the waiter over?

When I do finally flag down a waiter, I make a meal out of the order. Thanks to the pictures on the menu, I recognize some of the dishes, others are a complete mystery, and none seem like the right choice for a first meal of the day. I promise myself I will get more adventurous tomorrow, but for now I just need something resembling a Western breakfast so I can get to the supporters club a few doors over without any surprises in my belly. I order the club sandwich with french fries, and fear I'm turning into the ugly Canadian.

Waiting for my food to arrive, I catch a glimpse of myself in the floor-to-ceiling mirror directly to my right. It's the first time I've seen the sadness on my face. There's a gaunt and pale look to me; it looks like cluelessness mixed with defeat.

The plate arrives within minutes – which I think to myself is a little too quickly – and is essentially Spam covered in a strange salad dressing. Given the way I'm feeling about myself, I believe this to be exactly what I deserve. Eating by yourself is a lonely experience and a few forced bites into the disaster, I'm starting to well up again, in the middle of a restaurant full of strangers.

Fearing I might run into one of the Hong Kong Blues I'll be meeting later, I decide it's time to leave. I quickly pay at the front and notice the girl hands me back my credit card with two hands and a cute little bow. The concierge at the hotel did the same thing. Everything here feels weird.

With about an hour to kill before kick-off, I could pop into the British pub next to the restaurant, explore a little more of Wan Chai's streets or even just head to the supporters pub early for a beer. Instead I walk back to my hotel and take another 15 minutes to collect myself before walking back the exact same way I took just 90 minutes earlier: restaurant, strip club, British pub, repeat.

二月廿二日 星期六 曼城 對 史篤城 晚上 **11.00pm**

At 10.50pm I finally step into Maya Bar, a two-tiered open-concept pub located at 68–70 Lockhart Road, Wan Chai. The lower tier, which is at street level, houses the bar and the raised tier at the back is where the big screen TV sits and where the Hong Kong Blues congregate. I step up to the bar and order myself a beer.

I'm wearing a City top and the gentleman to my left takes exception.

'City are rubbish,' mutters a mid-40s man, with a west London accent.

'So who do you support?' I ask. I can tell he takes a moment to digest my 'American' accent before spitting out, 'QPR, mate!'

'I don't have any problem with QPR, in fact I think you'll find most City fans have a bit of a soft spot for them after 2012,' I reply with a cheeky wink and a grin.

'Fair enough,' he chuckles.

We chat for a bit about how great I thought the QPR fans were on the day City won the league, and about how happy he was to see the league go to City and not you-know-who. I make my way to the elevated back section of Maya, and the sight of some blue jerseys, the sound of Martin Tyler's voice belting Pellegrini's starting 11 over the house PA system and even the brief bit of banter with the QPR supporter has already lifted my spirits.

The back section of Maya can leave no doubt as to which team is supported here. The Hong Kong Blues banner stretches wall-to-wall, 'Hong Kong Blues, We're Not Really Here'. It's flanked by a framed picture of former City defender Sun Jihai and the prestigious Heart of the City award. Most of the Blues have already assembled by the time I arrive; they are about 40 strong on this Saturday night in Wan Chai, split pretty much 50/50 between locals and expats.

The first Blues I meet are Tom Derbyshire, the co-chair of the Hong Kong Blues, Mark Dale and his son Jack, and Phil Shirley with his son Thom. The two young lads are downing pints of Coke I'm sure will keep them up well past the 1am final whistle. After the very briefest of introductions, Tom disappears and returns with a Hong Kong Blues T-shirt and I'm well chuffed about it – Jesus, I'm even starting to speak Mancunian now.

A few minutes later the now-famous Marc Luk finally arrives, wearing a full-zip white City track top, matching hat, and a smile that could end civil wars. Like most Hong Kongers Marc looks much younger than his 33 years. He walks over and welcomes me to his home, but Marc's arrival at Maya Bar is greeted with such affection and enthusiasm among the Hong Kong Blues that I only get a brief moment with him before he has to make the rounds and say hello to all the regulars.

By this point I have fallen into a comfortable rhythm of: watch the first half, chat casually during half-time, then after the match really dig my teeth in and get to know the supporters. Tonight is different, however, as the first half is so painfully dull I'm worried this could be New York all over again – another dreadful 0-0 final against the Potters. I find myself looking for a chat and it doesn't take long before I spot an opportunity. In the tenth minute I spot a keeper jersey. And not just any keeper jersey, but a Kasper Schmeichel Thomas Cook-era keeper jersey. I *must* speak with this man.

Martin Ng stands about six feet tall, which I may have described as tall by Asian standards before my visit, but I'm quickly finding that stereotype, at least here in Hong Kong, to be largely untrue. Martin is also no lightweight, and I'd say he tips the scales somewhere around 220lb. Martin's smile is wider that any I've seen, the corners of his lips pushing his cheeks into round orbs, as he watches his heroes in blue race for loose balls on the big screen. I'm hesitant to interrupt such bliss.

'So, a Kasper Schmeichel jersey, you don't see a lot of those,' I say.

'Oh no, this is *Peter* Schmeichel. Kasper had a dad called Peter,' he replies.

Now, for those of you new to football or perhaps reading this book because you're related to me, a quick bit of history. Peter Schmeichel was arguably the best keeper who ever played for our crosstown rivals; you remember them, that team we beat 4-1 back in Chicago? Yeah, that bunch.

Near the end of old Peter's career he played one final season – for City. Peter made 29 appearances in goal during the 2002/03 season wearing the First Advice-sponsored jersey and his trademark number one. Peter's son Kasper then joined City from 2004–09, his final year spent wearing number 16 on the back of our Thomas Cook-sponsored shirt. This is the shirt Martin is wearing.

'My favourite player used to be Peter Schmeichel, I always loved keepers,' Martin continues. 'So when Peter came to City, I became City.'

'Wait a minute, you used to like United?' I ask, rather incredulously.

Martin wears a giant grin, which never leaves his face. He's the sort of person who looks like he's never been angry a day in his life.

'No, just Peter Schmeichel! But when he came to City, then I became City.'

By now, I've heard a million different ways people came to follow City, but this one is among the strangest. But as

I always say, whatever your introduction to City, all you need is that first taste and you're hooked. And as Martin pulls out his phone to proudly show me an autographed picture of Joe Hart, followed by another of Shay Given, I know he's had his taste and I know he's hooked. It was a strange path to City, but Martin is as 'City 'til I die' as they come. And he loves his keepers. But Martin, it still bears mentioning that your shirt is Kasper Schmeichel, not Peter.

The Stoke City versus Manchester City half-time arrives with a scoreline stuck on 0-0 and though we tell ourselves the game at the Etihad feels different from the one we drew away at the Britannia in September, none of us are convinced. As such the mood is somewhat reserved during the break.

I order up another beer and get chatting with the Hong Kong Blues' social media director Adnan Alghunaim, who moved to Hong Kong in 2012 to work with the Kuwaiti Ministry of Foreign Affairs. When choosing a Premier League team a few years back, Adnan decided he liked City's Arab connection and better still, the thought of winding up his cousin, who is a Red. There is also a Canadian connection with Adnan; he studied political science for three years at Carleton University, in my home province of Ontario. As we talk Rideau Canal and BeaverTails, another layer of homesickness peels away.

Down on the lower tier, a table of locals plays an intense card game I later learn is called Big Two. The four lads at the table appear so engrossed in their game that City could put seven past ex-Canadian Asmir Begovic tonight and I doubt they'd even notice.

I introduce myself and quickly learn their ringleader is Michael Wan. Michael wears the red and black striped City top and doesn't look a day over 30, yet Michael has already been a former police officer in Kensington and Chelsea and spent a great deal of his early life in Manchester, his aunt having owned a corner shop by Maine Road. No small mystery how Michael became City.

The second half begins and the longer it crawls forward, the more City appear destined for a 0-0 final – particularly after Dzeko misses an absolute sitter in front of a gaping goal. Maya is now jam-packed with City supporters clutching their pint glasses tightly, fiddling with their scarves and generally not saying too much. We remain all too aware that a draw to Stoke this late in the season could spell disaster for our title hopes. Only one supporter seems to be making much noise at all; I keep hearing one word being shouted, over and over again.

'Focus!'

The shouting comes from an unlikely source. Marc Luk.

Every time City turn the ball over, 'Focus!' When they win the ball back and go for a run, 'Focus!'

Even when nothing seems to be happening at all, 'Focus!'

When Alvaro Negredo is subbed out for Jovetic in the 56th minute, Marc has seen enough and he angrily throws his hat against the wall in protest.

I should have worn a hat. I bet it feels good to throw your hat against a wall.

Adnan leans in and whispers, 'We'll win for sure now, Marc is yelling, "focus".'

Each time Marc shouts 'focus' the other Blues respond in turn by shouting 'Focus, Marc, focus!' They aren't teasing Marc, rather this is some sort of tradition at Maya Bar – one I'm not quite getting yet.

Finally, in the 69th minute City's focus pays off. Kolarov whips a ball into the box just slightly behind the feet of

Yaya Touré, who stutter-steps and improvises the ball into the net. It didn't look pretty but it sure was beautiful. The Hong Kong Blues break into song and the singing won't stop until well after the final whistle; City 1, Stoke 0. We're back within three points of the title, and it's time for a little singing. The local Blues know every word to just about any City song you can name, past or present.

At 1am it is still early here in Wan Chai, so I go about my now customary routine of digging in and getting to know my fellow Blues. I get chatting with Greg Knowles who moved to Hong Kong from Wythenshawe 13 years ago and fell in love with the cosmopolitan and multicultural atmosphere. He tells me how son Alban's first match in September of 2004 was also his grandfather's last. You hear these sorts of landmark stories from Blues all the time, but they never get old or feel less emotional. Blues have an incredible appreciation for occasion, location, and family.

Tom Derbyshire moved here after working in Brunei and works as an English teacher. 'I wanted to make sure we also had a local chairman,' he tells me. 'I didn't want this to simply be an expats club, so I encouraged Marc to become my co-chairman.'

Their teamwork has yielded some notable results. The Hong Kong Blues, a club founded in 2010 by Graham Schofield, has gained worldwide recognition in less than four years. From meeting City players on tour, to pictures with the league trophy and a visit from the Brisbane Blues that no one here can stop talking about, Marc and Tom are the ideal chairmen.

Our waitress arrives carrying a tray of sambuca shots, and I can easily guess who ordered these.

'After meeting Peter Finch, I have to do sambuca shots after every City win,' Marc says.

He sets the four shots on fire and passes them around the cramped table to Michael Wan, Tom and me. The image of 60-something Tom Derbyshire, 30-somethings Marc Luk and Michael Wan, and myself doing flaming shots of sambuca is one for the ages. It is everything I hoped this journey would be about captured in shared blasts of Italian licorice. Marc downs his fireball, and his face quickly curls into itself. 'It's horrible, but then it's heaven!' he says.

Just before heading off, I meet Maya's owner, a late-30s Geordie named Chris Foalle, who arrived in 1995 when Hong Kong was still British and no working visas were required. Chris is yet another pub owner who supports a different club (Newcastle) but appreciates the patronage of the Blues. Oftentimes in Hong Kong, matches will kick off as early as 6am, but if Marc can get 12 people out, Chris will open the bar up at any time. Again, I love the Geordies.

I take one final look around Maya. Martin Ng, Mark Dale, Phil Shirley, Tom Derbyshire, Marc Luk, Adnan and Neil Mallalue, are still singing and dancing to 'Yaya, Kolo Touré', Michael Wan continues to dominate the game of Big Two. It's a perfect Saturday night in Wan Chai, a place that is feeling increasingly comfortable.

Marc asks me if I would like to grab a late dinner with him, which for me would be lunch. I'm absolutely famished after my failed attempt at breakfast and I'm not sure there has ever been a more welcome invitation.

香港

We arrive at a restaurant of Marc's choosing just steps from both Maya and the first restaurant I tried and sit down over an appreciated plate of delicious white fish and rice.

'So did you know my wife and I stayed with Peter Finch on the Isle of Wight?' Marc begins.

'Yes, he told me. Did you go to the Horseshoe Pub?' I ask excitedly.

'Oh yes, we drank many sambuca there!'

'Did you get to a match?' I ask.

'Yes, later in the week Peter took me and my wife up to Manchester for our first Premier match! It was the game where we beat Chelsea 1-0 and Tevez scored the winner, which was great because my wife supports Chelsea. Peter got us hospitality access and I met Tony Book, Ian Brightwell and Joe Corrigan. When Joe entered the room he said, "I hear we have a special visitor all the way from Hong Kong, please welcome Marc Luk." Joe Corrigan said my name – I couldn't believe it! Peter Finch changed my life; I really believe I was destined to meet him.'

Writing is often a lonely endeavour and a great dinner companion can make all the difference in the world. As Marc and I trade stories over dinner, and I rapid-fire some of my burning questions his way, the sadness I was experiencing begins to leave for good.

'Why are floors four and 14 missing in the elevators?' I ask.

'Because in Chinese the word for "four" sounds very close to the word for "death".'

'There was this old lady trying to drag me into a strip joint at Luard Road and Lockhart, at least I think it was a strip joint, was it a strip joint?'

'Yes. And unless you can spare a thousand pounds on your credit card, never go in there,' Marc warns.

I am beginning to realize what has been causing me to feel off: loneliness. My original career in music was probably the least-lonely job on the planet, and though it pays about the same as writing, the similarities pretty much end there. Not having someone else to share the immediacy of the incredible sights and people I keep experiencing along this journey has resulted in an intense feeling of loneliness. But here with Marc I am able to unload, and I'm finally feeling like me again.

'Did you hear me shouting "focus" during the match?' Marc asks.

'Yes! I've been meaning to ask you what that's all about. I've even got it written here in my notes, look,' I point to the entry in my black notebook, my gift from the Redondo Beach Blues now nearing the end of its ride.

'Well, the day I went to the Chelsea match with Peter Finch, I was so nervous and excited and surrounded by all these lifelong City fans and legends, I didn't know what I should be saying or doing. All of a sudden in the second half I just yelled, "focus!"'

Marc appears as baffled as I do as to its meaning.

'But shortly after shouting it, Tevez scored and now I can't stop saying it, it's our lucky word. If the match is close, Tom Derbyshire and everyone else at Maya like to shout, "Marc, focus!"'

The following afternoon I traipse all over Wan Chai, feeling completely reinvigorated. I snap as many pictures as my camera will hold before sprinting back to the hotel to dump them into my computer and head back out for more. Pictures of packed-out basketball courts, old women practising tai chi, the Frank Gehry-designed Opus building that looks like it grew out of the side of the mountain in three separate directions, and pictures of signs with amusing English translations.

If I came into Hong Kong feeling homesick and lonely, I leave here absolutely buzzing.

Focus. Too damn right.

11
ALKRINGTON AND REDDISH

Fanzone

I ARRIVE in Manchester still buzzing from Hong Kong. The flight back was a breeze and we even stopped off in Amsterdam long enough for a burger, chips with mayo, and a giant bottle of Heineken. With five days to go before City's League Cup Final match I have scheduled two quick midweek stops: the monthly meetings of the Alkrington Blues on Tuesday, and a long-awaited trip to the Reddish branch the following day.

Let's begin at The Lancashire Fold, 77 Kirkway in Alkrington – not Altrincham, or Accrington – a small borough in Middleton. Alkrington is a relatively new branch formed just last season by chairman Rick Slater and committee member Mark Oldham.

There won't be matches to watch at these two meetings. The majority of these supporters are season-ticket holders and attend all home matches and travel on coaches to most of the away ones. As such it is standard practice among the English-based supporters clubs to hold a monthly meeting to discuss all matters relating to the club. These meetings usually include invited City personalities who act as liaisons between the club and supporters. My invite came from Mark, just before I left for Hong Kong, and was of particular interest due to one of this evening's scheduled guests.

'FanZone' Danny Jackson rose to prominence and City folklore one magical day in February 2008, on a television show called *FanZone*. The now-defunct programme followed a simple premise: stick two bitter enemies in a sound booth, each with a microphone, and film them live as they watch the rival teams face off against one another. When Benjani scored at Old Trafford against United to put City ahead 2-0, Danny's delirious celebration call of 'Two nil up at the swamp!' became an instant classic and is a phrase still used today in the increasingly common event City take a 2-0 lead at Old Trafford.

Danny is joined by Natalie Pike, a well-known model in the UK and a born-and-raised Blue. Natalie hosts the live matchday events along with Danny in City Square, and the two have remarkable chemistry. They are as sharp, knowledgeable and entertaining as anyone I've yet met at City and for nearly an hour they have the room full of Alkrington Blues hanging on their every word.

I share a table with 71-year-old Clive Rubin, his wife, Glynn, and their lifelong friends John and Andy, the latter returning to the table with a full round of drinks just as Danny and Natalie take to the mic.

Two gentlemen introducing themselves as Steve and Craig sit down at the table to my left, and both offer to buy me a pint. I tell them I'll take something local and Steve returns with a gorgeous pint of JW Lee's bitter as we settle in for the meeting. Every time Danny or Natalie throw out an answer to a member's question, Clive has a witty reply of his own.

It is here in Alkrington where I begin to grasp what a headache the chairman's job can be. Rick Slater and Mark Oldham calmly explain to the supporters that City have only granted them four of the 51 Barcelona away tickets they applied for. The only fair thing to do is put everyone's name in a raffle and tell the supporters to cross their fingers.

Next, a warning for those travelling to Wembley for the cup final, 'For those of you who think you have time for a pint before the bus leaves: you do *not* have time for a pint after the match; you *will* miss the bus like last time.'

After the guest speakers have finished and the monthly meeting has wrapped up, I stick around with Clive and his gang for a bit of pub trivia, hanging out with people twice my age – interesting, but not at all awkward.

'Do you have a girl back home?' Glynn asks.

'Yes, yes I do.'

'And how long have you been courting your girlfriend?'

I need a brief moment to try and recall exactly what constitutes courting, before replying, 'About two years now.'

'Make sure you write her something every day, or else she might chuck you!'

A rather ominous warning from someone who has lived two of my lifetimes. Advice worth considering.

The end of my evening in Alkrington is spent with Andy Logan, chatting about his beloved Green Bay Packers. As Andy runs through his expert analysis of the past NFL season, I find myself wondering if my Canadian accent when discussing English football sounds as bizarre as Andy's does talking American football.

Alkrington and Reddish

The night after Alkrington I make my first visit to the famous Reddish Blues. In 1997, lifelong best mates Mark Wood and Tim Bramley decided they needed better access to away tickets. When they learned the best way to achieve this was to become a member of a supporters club, they, along with Howard Burr, formed a club in their home borough of Reddish.

With Bramley in Redondo Beach and Woody in Toronto, Howard Burr has taken the lead at the club, and 17 years after its formation, as Woody once humbly admitted to me, 'Hand on heart, Howard has taken the Reddish Blues to a height me and Tim likely would never have reached.'

In Bramley and Woody's day, the club would meet at The Carousel, but Howard has since moved the Reddish Blues' 424 members to The Houldsworth Working Men's Club, better known as 'The Big Club' to the locals. A working men's club is essentially just that, a pub designated for blue-collar workers, permitted to serve drinks at a cheaper price.

The Houldsworth Working Men's Club looks precisely the way you're imagining; its old wood panelling along the walls, stale maroon carpet and cigarette-yellowed ceilings reminding me fondly of the local legion halls back home in Canada.

In Reddish, the guests are Andy Morrison, hero and captain of the 1999 City squad that lifted us out of the Third Division; Alex Williams, an enormous man who was City's number one keeper in the early-to-mid-'80s; and Paul Lake.

Paul's book *I'm Not Really Here* about his years of struggling through injury, is not only one of the best Man City books ever written, it is widely considered one of the best football books ever written. I met Lakey in Toronto a year previous on the famous evening he and Dan Reynolds arranged for the Premier League trophy to come to Opera Bob's, but it is still a tremendous thrill when he sits down beside me.

'Hey Darryl, mate, how's everything? You know, I had a great breakfast with Dan Reynolds a few weeks back, how's he getting on in Tel Aviv?'

'He's loving it. Might never come back,' I answer.

'And what about Woody? What a great guy, I remember meeting him in Toronto. He's from around these parts you know, our daughters used to go to swimming together.'

Lakey is sharp. He never forgets a face, a name, nor the relevance of that face and name. Needless to say, when I relay this message to Woody the following day, he's over the moon that his favourite City player of all time was asking about him.

The part in my Reddish evening that sticks with me the most is the fans' ability to air their grievances to Paul, Andy and Alex. The main concern for Reddish Blues at the moment is the encroachment of corporate seating, bumping long-time season ticket holders from their current seats to less desirable locations. Andy Morrison promises to look into it and I believe that he is the sort of man who will do just that, but the Scotsman doesn't pull any punches, 'If you want to compete and see the results we've been seeing, it means more corporate seating.'

We don't have a forum of this level in North American sports: intimate monthly access to former legends, who are genuinely concerned and who act as a direct liaison between supporter and club.

The nights in Alkrington and Reddish were welcoming, insightful and entirely enjoyable. But the highlight of the two comes at the very end of my evening at Houldsworth Working Men's Club. Howard Burr, the middle-aged father of two grown children, stops me just before I'm out the door.

'Be back here for 5.30am on Sunday. The coach leaves at 6am sharp,' Howard says.

Howard hands me an envelope. I open it up to find another envelope, sky blue, with white letters, 'Capital One Cup'.

'You're with us,' he says.

Reddish Blues

12
WEMBLEY

Typical City

THE ALARM on my cellphone has somehow managed to cut through the sound of the wailing car alarms outside my sister's flat. I'm pawing wildly for my mobile, looking like Mike Tyson searching for his mouth guard after Buster Douglas knocked it halfway across the ring back in '90.

What is different about this 5.30am from the Isle of Wight 5.30am is; I set this alarm, I am not hung-over, and it was my full intention to awake at this ungodly hour.

5.30am is all I've been thinking about in the days since Howard handed me that ticket. Never mind that Jess and I might be on our last legs, just as Clive's wife warned. Forget that I'm broke and disregard the notion that my passport might still derail any future stops. Today Darryl Webster, from East Gwillimbury, Ontario, goes to Wembley and I refuse to let any other thoughts occupy my mind.

I catch a taxi outside of my sister's building. It's still dark out as the cab cuts through the drizzle and the blackness on our way to Stockport. Here, the streetlights glow a deeper and warmer yellow than in North America. I don't know why, and I'm not interested in finding out, I just like that they do, and that's worth mentioning.

I arrive back at Houldsworth Working Men's Club at 5.45am on Sunday 2 March. Three massive coaches sit parked at the ready; a fourth is late arriving. I jump in the first one, marked 'Reddish Coach A' with Howard, and grab a seat up near the front. Howard, usually full of energy and boundless optimism, doesn't seem himself this morning and wears a particular shade of green on his face that clashes badly with his sky-blue track jacket.

'Howard, mate, were you out on the piss last night?' I ask.

'No, pal, I woke up at two this morning with the chills and well, you know, something else,' he confides, gently rubbing his stomach.

Poor Howard Burr, on the day of the Capital One Cup Final, has an old-fashioned case of the trots – not something you want on a four-hour ride to London on a coach with a broken toilet.

As we pull out, I can't help but marvel at our driver's ability to navigate the giant 50-seater coach through Reddish's tiny streets, flanked by red-brick Victorian-era buildings and tidy row-houses painted over the canvas of Stockport.

As we make our way out of Reddish towards the motorway I find myself wondering which house was Woody's; where did he and Tim first meet; which off-licence did they use to try and blag tins of lager from before they were old enough? Which tiny cul-de-sac did the taxi drop them off at on the famous night they had a drunken fight that woke up all the neighbours outside Woody and Jeanette's first house together?

As we reach the Reddish border en route to my first cup final, I'm struck by the disproportionate number of take-away shops. There would appear to be a take-away of some sort for every 15 residents of Reddish. I never did see a grocery store, but Woody assures me there's at least one Asda near the edge of town.

We make a brief pit stop at Warwick services where Howard's daughter Katy loads him up on over-the-counter meds. As we draw nearer to London, scores of cars, trucks and minibuses stream by our coach with City scarves and flags fighting to stretch out and show themselves against the violent speed of the motorway. My excitement grows with every half-mile, and from each passing slip road, another fleet of vehicles joins the Blue armada to Wembley.

By 11am we're in London and I get my first glimpse of a coach carrying today's rivals from Sunderland. As we sit idle at a red light, the coach full of red-and-white-clad Black Cats drives directly past us, the sight of our coach causing each and every supporter on their coach to press against the windows like taunting, ravenous animals.

It is in this moment that I realize there will be 40,000 of these maniacs inside the stadium and occupying the surrounding streets I am about to frequent.

Howard instructs our coach driver to tuck us into a tidy little side alley that he knows has a quick post-match escape route. If this is my first trip to Wembley, Howard – having travelled here four times in the past 18 months – may as well be a steward at Wembley, such is his knowledge of the landscape.

Our rendezvous point with the other three Reddish coaches is a Wetherspoon pub, a well-known chain of over-sized British pubs. The streets of Wembley are teeming with City blue and Sunderland red. The occasion thus far is affable, but the security guards outside of each pub still know better than to mix supporters. As we step into our Wetherspoon, we discover a gesticulating mass of sky blue set against a drunken cacophony of City chants.

The Reddish Blues have kindly provided my passage to and from Britain's capital, and I in turn offer to order up the first round of drinks for our clique of Fran Ahern, Howard and Katy Burr, Brian Jackson, Paul Diggett, Chris Roche, Peter Garlick and Gordon Garlick, who, though I press him early and often, swears no relation to Chicago's Warren Garlick – but who would ever admit to being Warren's kin?

The line to reach the bar is at least eight rows deep and it takes me over 20 minutes to get served, which, when measured against a significant thirst for lager, feels more like 90. I finally team up with a random Blue I've made friends with in line and we get our orders in. Howard has decided to tempt fate with a pint of bitter on his dodgy tummy and daughter Katy has asked me to grab her something called a 'Blue Wicked', apparently good for a hangover.

After my seemingly eternal wait for alcohol, I'm pretty certain we'll only get one pint in before the match, such is the crush at the bar. This is, until I discover that Fran and Brian have hidden two pitchers in the decorative fake tree placed in the corner of the pub in which we've assembled. Genius! Two pints is exactly what the doctor ordered before making our final march towards Wembley.

We exit the pub to discover southern streets overrun with northerners. City blue mixes with Sunderland red and white, seemingly without incident.

'I prefer this to playing United at Wembley,' Howard confesses.

'Why's that? Wouldn't you love to watch City beat them *here*?'

'I saw it in 2011 at the FA Cup semi-final. The atmosphere was all wrong. Too intense for me.'

Howard carefully studies Mancs and Mackems mixing in all corners, funnelling towards Wembley, exuberance and a great sense of occasion outweighing any aggression.

'I'll take this over hostility any day. My nerves can't handle derbies anyways,' he says.

I consider Howard's already dodgy stomach and with that in mind I think everyone on our coach is happy this isn't a derby.

Unfortunately, as the Wembley trip was short notice, the Reddish Blues weren't able to secure me a ticket in their section, and as we reach Entrance R, I must say a temporary goodbye to the rest of the gang.

Sunday 2 March. League Cup Final. City v Sunderland, 2pm kick-off

As I rise up escalator after escalator, only to discover another escalator, I wonder if the third tier of this stadium is simply a rumour. The giant walls beside the escalator are all glass and you can see the supporters lined up outside. Two proud 1894 flags – representing a unique supporters group dedicated to the preservation of Man City culture – wave proudly above thousands of City supporters lined up to get in.

When I finally arrive at the top tier, excitement has full control of my guts. If I don't find my section and see the pitch soon I will burst.

The three other supporters on the stairs in front of me at block 544 cause the final few steps to feel like an eternity, knowing I'm inches from laying eyes on one of football's most famous stadiums.

As I finally make my way past two hulking stewards, Wembley is revealed to me for the first time. Waking up at 5.30am and driving four hours on a coach, waiting 30 minutes for a pint, all a laughable price to pay for what my eyes land upon. I'm early enough that I can still see W-E-M-B-L-E-Y spelled out in the empty seats at the opposite end, as if the Sunderland supporters somehow knew this would be an innocent Canadian's first time here, and decided they'd leave their seats empty until I arrived.

After 20 minutes of taking in the immensity of Wembley from my vantage point in row 11, seat 145 – and after eating the largest hot dog I've ever had – a burst of orange fireworks envelops the pitch signalling the players' arrival. The stands are now full, cut exactly down the middle – 45,000 Blues, 45,000 Red-and-Whites – and the two clubs are prepared to do battle for the first trophy of the season: the League Cup.

I've been to big American football stadiums before, and I've watched a match at Camp Nou. But nothing compares to seeing your club at Wembley. It is, I imagine, football's equivalent of ballet at the Bolshoi.

Ten minutes in, an uncharacteristic misstep from Vincent Kompany allows Fabio Borini to charge in alone on Joe Hart. The Italian striker takes full advantage and smashes his laces into the ball, England's number-one keeper helpless to stop it. Sunderland 1 City 0. From my vantage point in the third tier, above City's corner flag, the Sunderland supporters resemble kernels bursting out of a popcorn machine that's lost its lid.

In the section directly to my right, about ten ill-advised Sunderland supporters have managed to find a ticket in the City end. The antagonists rise from their seats, reveal their opposing colours and begin to overzealously celebrate their team's goal. If you think this is something that went over well with the Blues in block 543 then you haven't followed much football.

I must say that if hooliganism or football violence in some strange way appealed to me in my early 20s (what testosterone-charged man in his 20s wasn't attracted to a bit of aggression?) each passing year has removed another level of violence's appeal. Two months shy of 37, I can firmly say I've come to abhor violent football supporters. Every part of me wants to say City are the exception to football's stereotype. I want to believe that when it comes to City, supporters need not be segregated, but on this day, in this moment, I am all too aware that we, as well as Sunderland, can be guilty at times.

A fight quickly breaks out and one Sunderland fan in particular is pummelled mercilessly. The fact that these Nobel laureates from Sunderland decided to sit in the City section is one form of idiocy; the fact that they chose to sit in the middle of the row is an entirely greater folly. The stewards at Wembley are having a difficult time getting through the mayhem to break up the melee, none of the Blues in a particular rush to help.

City enter the half down 1-0 and the mood is very much one of 'Typical City', an attitude City supporters have come to adopt after decades of near-victories turned into shattering defeats. Sunderland is a team at the bottom of the table, seemingly destined for relegation, yet here we are on England's biggest stage, shitting the bed.

I meet up with Chris Nield in the concourse; he and Ian are sitting in the section where the trouble kicked off. I ask Chris if he is okay and if he was near any of the punches. Nieldy, a vegetarian, yoga enthusiast and generally one of the most non-violent people I've ever known, seems entirely unfazed by the brawl. But then again Chris also grew up a lifelong Blue in early-'90s Droylsden, so fights such as these are water off a duck's back for Nieldy.

I quickly realize we have a second half to focus on. Chris doesn't seem too worried about the scoreline at the moment; he's witnessed comebacks before at Wembley. In 1999, the old Wembley – near the end of its storied run, battered and broken down – hosted the famous Third Division Play-Off Final against Gillingham, in which City stormed back from 2-0 down to draw level in injury time before winning promotion on penalties and capturing the imagination of a young Joey McCune. The famous victory catapulted City back into the second tier of English football.

Most supporters I have met here in England were there that day and most point to the match as the turning point in City's revival. So with that in mind, and Chris's assurances that this match is far from over, I grab a hot cup of tea – to warm against what has suddenly become a chilly March evening – and settle back into row 11, seat 145, for the second half.

If the first half was a display of the old City and old football violence, the second half is a welcome opposite. Yaya Touré, my mother's favourite Ivorian, hits a one-timer of a fancy pass from Pablo Zabaleta, which from our angle looks like it is sailing well high and wide of the goal. It isn't. It's only when the knotted twine bulges behind a desperately stretched Vito Mannone that we realize City have levelled 1-1. Time for the Blue half of Wembley to go mental.

We've hardly stopped singing when, next, Samir Nasri, with a nearly identical one-time hit, curls his shot inside the far post. High fives and hugs abound in a section full of people I've never met, such is the hysteria and amity produced by going up 2-1 at Wembley.

Finally in the 90th minute, an unlikely scorer rockets down the pitch towards our section and fires the final shot in the League Cup, and I wonder to myself if young Ellis Woods, the future superstar I met in Toronto, might be here in London, wearing his hero's shirt, Jesus having just put the outcome out of the question. For the second time in my life I watch City lift a trophy, and given the scenic backdrop it feels every bit as surreal as the first.

Reddish and Wembley

On the walk back to the coach, the Sunderland fans and City fans mingle as one; the ten or so troublemakers who scarred the proceedings early on are the exception more than the rule. The Sunderland fans as a whole are tremendous, so good in fact that the newspapers in Manchester write about them the following day, just as the papers in Sunderland write about City's admirable support. It is widely agreed by all who were here today that Manchester City would happily play Sunderland, and interact with their supporters in the streets of London, any time.

As we reach our coach, Howard, a few steps ahead of me, is welcomed by a group of Sunderland supporters, leaned against their Hummer limousine. 'Alright Howard! Congratulations, mate,' one of them shouts.

Howard walks over and shakes hands before climbing on to his coach and counting heads, once again putting the welfare of his friends first and a dodgy stomach second. With all the Blues on Coach A accounted for, we head off up the road back to Manchester.

You might think watching your club come from behind to lift a cup at Wembley would be one of life's great highlights, and you would be right. But for me, it wasn't even the most memorable part of that day. From this day until my last day, when I look back on 2 March 2014, my most vivid and fond memory will be of a coach ride back to Reddish.

On the ride down, there was talk of a 'disco party' on the way back, but as the tired and weary Blues of Reddish climbed back on to the coach, having been up since 5.30am with a few lagers in between, this promise seems unlikely.

Twelve-year-old star in the making Josh Moore gets on the bus PA system somewhere around Watford and bellows out, 'The disco will commence at 6.45pm sharp!' The coachful of half-asleep Blues chuckle and seem to humour young Josh, younger looking than his 12 years, but far wiser-sounding. This group of adult Blues appears all but ready for their beds and back to work in the morning. As I gaze back from the front row, I look down the bus at the 20 or so rows behind me. We're anywhere from 12 to 70 years old, but the majority are north of 40. There won't be any disco here tonight, I'm sure of it.

At 6.45pm sharp, young Josh returns to the mic, 'Alright everyone, time to get off yer bums and start dancing.'

I feel badly for Josh, try as he may, he simply can't understand when adults have had enough for one day. The opening drum fill to Candi Staton's 1976 hit 'Young Hearts' kicks in, followed by the horn section. The Heron family – Jim, Bev and daughter Casey – lead the charge and by the time Miss Staton belts out 'Young hearts, run free', to my sheer amazement a coachful of 50 exhausted Blues spring from their seats and form a disco-conga line that dances up and down the aisles of the bus and won't stop until we're back in Reddish.

I look over to Howard, across the aisle; weary, dodgy-stomached and smiling ear-to-ear.

'Exactly like the ride home last year,' he says.

Which is hard to believe considering last year they were coming home from a shock defeat to massive underdogs Wigan. Or maybe it isn't hard to believe. Maybe, as I am beginning to understand, this is all just typical City.

Howard finally closes his eyes and drifts into a peaceful and well-earned kip, as his Reddish Blue army dance late into the evening on a coach bound for Manchester.

13
GIBRALTAR

New Kids On The Rock

LANDINGS OFTEN appear perilous: one moment there is no runway in sight and then before you know it, land comes into view, offering a necessary measure of calming perspective. Still, as Monarch Airlines flight 574 makes its final approach into Gibraltar, the woman to my immediate right is doing her best to make me question what I know, and is more than just rattling my nerves.

She peeks quickly out of her window, before whipping her head around to expose her petrified face to my side of the aisle, a face that seems to be asking her friend on my side, 'Can you see the runway?' This woman, despite having two perfectly good hands, chooses instead to point with her face, which only adds to her desperation. Her pointing face, searching desperately for land, begs for reassurance, but our side of the plane can't offer any; all we can see are whitecaps getting closer by the half-second.

If she can't see land from her side, where the hell is it? Where is this big rock already?

Mark Guy, whom I'll (hopefully) meet in about 15 minutes, neglected to tell me RAF Gibraltar is widely considered among the world's most dangerous airports to land at. Perhaps Mark knew that given this information I might have chosen a visit to Jersey or the Costa Blanca over Gibraltar.

A pilot gets one shot at Gibraltar: if she or he decides it's too windy and aborts the landing, that plane is immediately sent to Malaga. It's windy this morning and our pilot would be forgiven for aborting, but this maverick wants it bad, and we're coming in hot. Just as I believe I could reach out the window and scoop a handful of warm saline water from the Strait of Gibraltar, I see a pebble, then a rock, followed by the thump of wheels down. The brakes are slammed on as hard as I've ever felt them in a plane and we come to a full stop, seemingly just inches from Morocco.

The passengers let out a collective exhale as laughs ripple through the cabin, the experienced locals getting a kick out of the scared-shitless first-timers.

After kissing the tarmac and clearing Gibraltar customs – which was essentially a 'Good morning', Gibraltar sharing the same passport requirements as the UK – I step outside and meet my host, Mark Guy.

'I thought for sure I'd be collecting you from Malaga today,' Mark says.

'I'd have been okay with that,' I reply.

Mark wears his hair shaved to the lowest clip, a look I am now convinced is the official haircut of OSC chairmen. I would very much like to take a group picture some day featuring: Mark Guy, Mark Mulvanny, Howard Burr and Tim Bramley and have readers guess who is who.

I like to think I knew where Gibraltar was before deciding to come here – the bottom of Spain, essentially. Sure I think I knew that. I think I also knew it was British territory, hotly contested with Spain.

So in essence I arrive in Gibraltar knowing almost nothing and as such am quite eager to discover this ancient world. The first thing you notice about the tiny British overseas territory is, of course, the famous Rock, captured by the British from the Spanish in 1704. The Rock of Gibraltar towers imposingly over the landscape, sheer white rock face on one side; sparse foliage reminiscent of the Hollywood Hills adorns the opposite side.

The second thing I notice is a curiosity entirely unique to Gibraltar. The main street in Gibraltar literally intersects the airport's runway; I've never seen anything like it. When a plane is coming in, giant barriers, similar to those that would signal a train crossing, come down and block jet from pedestrian. With the next arrival into Gibraltar still an hour away, Mark and I look both ways before crossing the runway and head over to his apartment.

Along the way to Mark's place we stroll past what is, for now, Gibraltar's national stadium. Gibraltar has just been recognized by UEFA and will begin qualifiers for Euro 2016 in less than a year from now. Work has begun on a new stadium, in a part of the country we'll visit a little later. I arrived nice and early having caught the four-hour flight to Gibraltar at 7am from Manchester and by midday we've dropped my bags off and navigated a few narrow streets of cobblestone to Mark's favourite Moroccan take-away. We both order a Moroccan-Anglo fusion of thin steak and chips. I add a small salad to my order; Mark, ever the Mancunian, isn't interested in any veg. We pull two small metal chairs up to a matching table, the aroma of Moroccan beef so arresting, we both have bites before bums hit seats.

'I'm supposed to be on a diet,' Mark says, digging in chips first. 'You'll be meeting my missus later on. Don't tell her about this.'

'Your secret's safe with me, mate,' I assure him, if only for the duration of my visit.

A breeze sweeps through the narrow alley and relieves me of my untethered serviette. I watch as it dances away from our table past shop windows and attractive olive-skinned women. There is a hum, a soundtrack to these streets, an unlikely world orchestra of Moroccan, Spanish and British.

'So, was your dad City?' I ask.

'No, mate, my dad has no clue about football,' Mark mumbles through another mouthful of lunch.

'Your mum then?'

'Nope.'

'So how did you become City then?'

'I was five at the time.' Mark puts his fork down and wipes the corner of his smile. 'I'd come off my bike and broke my arm quite badly, to the point it had to be broken again and reset. The next morning, my godfather Andy Handford, who is a huge Blue, came for a visit.'

Mark extends his arm, and traces his finger from shoulder to wrist, 'He decided to write Manchester City down the cast. And from that day onwards, I was a Blue.'

Morocco's influence is everywhere in Gibraltar and I find my heart aching to take the ferry over.

'How far are we from Morocco?' I ask.

'Come on, I'll show you.'

As Mark and I wait at the bottom of the Rock, to catch Gibraltar's free bus, a Barbary ape runs directly across our path and darts towards the pub across the street. After the Rock, Barbary apes – which are tailless monkeys – are probably the second-best-known part of Gibraltar.

Legend has it that as long as there are Barbary apes in Gibraltar, the Rock will remain in British hands. It was with this in mind that Winston Churchill ordered more apes be shipped in from Algeria and Morocco during WWII, the population dwindling and the Nazis hell-bent on capturing the gateway to North Africa.

Our bus ride – a winding and treacherous ten minutes through the hills along a narrow one-lane road, which somehow manages to facilitate both directions of traffic – brings us to Europa Point. The point is Gibraltar's most southern tip and provides an unmatched view of the Bay of Gibraltar, Spain and Morocco.

Standing in a place where three countries and two continents are in view of the naked eye, I can finally appreciate why this place has been so hotly contested throughout history and still today. One giant cannon symbolically guards the Rock, the prominent Ibrahim-al-Ibrahim Mosque, the church, the lighthouse and soon, Gibraltar's new national stadium.

I can't imagine matches being played here, such is the intensity of the swirling wind, seeming to hit me from every direction. Corner kicks will surely blow into the strait and wash out into the Mediterranean. With Gibraltar being drawn into a group with world heavyweights Germany, seeing the likes of Thomas Muller and Mesut Ozil playing here will be nothing if not interesting, and for the locals, an enormous point of pride.

On the short bus ride back into town, Mark confesses he is struggling with what he calls PMT.

'Pre Match Tension, mate. My stomach is in knots.'

'I'd say you can relax, 2-0 down to Barcelona at home isn't something we're likely to come back from,' I reply.

And even though this is my answer, I can't shake this romantic notion that City might pull off a win for the ages tonight. But Mark's nerves are apparent enough that I don't want to do anything to further the thought this could be a historic win.

'Stranger things have happened pal; I was at the Tottenham FA Cup match in '04,' Mark says.

The match to which Mark is referring is one of City's most famous come-from-behind victories in club history.

'I went to London with my mate Paul Blackshaw. We were down 3-0 at the half *and* Joey Barton had been sent off, so we were down three goals with only ten men. I told Paul that we could make it back to the hotel, get our bags and catch the last train back to Manchester rather than staying the night in north London. Paul said, "No, let's stay, it will be okay."

'So we stayed. Couple minutes in to the restart Distin scores. Couple minutes after that, Paul Bosvelt gets a deflection, 3-2. But we're still down a man and thinking surely Tottenham are going to get another on the counter-attack. Ten minutes to play, Shaun Wright-Phillips scores and we're all square. And then in added time, Jon Macken with a header for the ages. Next thing you know, we're getting a message from Paul's daughter saying we can see you jumping up and down on telly!'

Now, if only tonight's Barcelona were 2004's Tottenham. Mind you, tonight's Manchester City is a world apart from 2004's club. And again I've convinced myself we have a shot. And now I have PMT.

Wednesday 12 March. Champions League Round of 16. Barcelona v City. 8.45pm kick-off

After the largest Indian meal I've ever enjoyed, at a restaurant named Charlie's, Mark, his wife Karen, her son J.J. and I make the brief 90-second walk next door to Champions Bar and Grill, Unit 2B, The Tower, Marina Bay, Gibraltar where, for the moment, the Gibraltar Blues have been congregating.

Champions is a Euro-take on North American sports bars: big TVs and chicken wings mixed with white booth seating more akin to a dance club. By the end of the season, the Gib Blues will have moved to a more traditional British pub, the Trafalgar, closer to the Rock, and directly across from where I saw my first Barbary ape.

Mark started the Gib Blues because it was the best way to apply for tickets as an away supporter or when visiting home for a match. The Gibraltar Blues have taken full advantage of this perk as most of them have made the ten-hour drive to Barcelona this evening. Mark's work is keeping him in town for tonight and along with James 'Gingy' Alker, we make up the only Blues in a decidedly pro-Barcelona bar.

Twenty-year-old Josh, who wears his fiery red hair in a pony tail, is spending his last night in Gibraltar – before moving back to England – cheering on the Blues before starting his final night shift with William Hill. Gibraltar's taxes, or lack thereof, have created a haven for online gambling companies.

Early into the match, some Red trolls who have come out tonight to cheer against City make a sad attempt at taunting us.

'City are going out tonight!' is the best one muppet can come up with.

'At least we're going out to the best team in the world. You lot are going out to Olympiakos tomorrow,' replies young James.

Ultimately United will manage to just scrape by Olympiakos tomorrow, but in this moment it looks as though they're headed out to the Greek champions, and it's a crafty retort. By tomorrow James and I will both be back in Manchester, where we're certain to never run into these Reds again.

City head into tonight's match needing a 2-0 result just to force extra time, Barcelona having done us by that score at the Etihad two weeks ago. The match kicks off up the road in Barcelona, and the PMT sets in for the three of us; J.J. more interested in throwing darts, Karen, a Liverpool supporter, happy to sip rosé and laugh at her nervous husband.

Despite a narrowly missed header, Barcelona dominate City, who manage to hold the fort for 60 minutes, but simply holding the fort isn't going to do. In the 67th minute Lionel Messi, the greatest footballer in a generation, puts the Catalan giants up 1-0 and with only 25 minutes left, we know there's no coming back from this one.

Still, I'm not the least bit disappointed that most of the Gibraltar Blues are in Barcelona while we're sitting here, just three of us in a pub full of rival supporters. It's a nice change of pace from previous clubs in which I felt a great responsibility to speak with as many supporters as possible, often at the expense of my liver. Tonight I settle in with Mark and James and enjoy discussing things such as: have we brought Aguero back too early from injury? And just how lucky we are to be alive to witness Lionel Messi in his prime.

Gibraltar

Tonight's defeat isn't the sort of loss that leaves you gutted, rather it leaves you dreaming that one day City could reach the heights of a team like Barcelona, and excited that for the first time in 40 years, this appears a plausible near-future for the boys in blue. The 'this could never be us' thinking replaced by a far more hopeful, 'this *will* be us'.

As Mark and I walk back to his apartment, he speaks longingly of Manchester and his son Sam. Mark speaks of Sam non-stop and I wish I had the experience to contribute to a conversation about a divorced father who misses his son. The best I can offer is my ear, though even this is proving difficult as Gibraltar at night is hard to ignore: the Rock against the moonlight, the smell of Moroccan food and a breeze from the Strait of Gibraltar winding through the tiny side streets as though it was searching for me.

I would have loved to stay longer in Gibraltar and jump the ferry to Tangiers just like a proper author. But my luck with the passport has finally run out. There will be no Morocco this time. If I'm to have any chance of making Abu Dhabi, I need to go home and renew this document.

The next morning Mark walks me back to the airport and we say our goodbyes, feeling much more like age-old friends than two men who met 24 hours previous.

'Thanks for everything, mate, it was well worth shitting myself on that landing,' I say.

'Mate, forget the landing; take-off is far worse.'

14
THE PASSPORT ISSUE

INSTEAD OF the ferry to Tangiers, I hop on a plane to Birmingham. From there my mate Karl McNelly drives me back to Manchester, before getting drunk and falling into the fountain outside of my sister's flat. The following morning Karl wakes up late for his flight to Germany but, thanks to a surreal layer of morning fog covering the whole of Manchester in a giant blanket, makes it to Manchester Airport in time. And thanks to a minor miracle at the death, I'll be just a few hours behind him en route to a place I've long dreamed of visiting.

A few weeks earlier, around about the time of Hong Kong, I received an email from Etihad Airways about the possibility of a free flight to Abu Dhabi. The airline and I emailed back and forth a few times and finally, after what I suspect was a slightly embellished endorsement from Chris Nield, Etihad offered me a round-trip flight from Manchester to Abu Dhabi with the agreement I will write about a team of coaches City are sending to the UAE for a series of clinics.

Sorted, right? Not so fast.

My passport – now with only 98 days remaining before it expires – has finally caught up with me. To get into Abu Dhabi, you require six months' validity on your passport; there is absolutely no way around this rule.

If Etihad don't agree to fly me from Toronto to Abu Dhabi instead of from Manchester, that will be the end of the ride, and I will fall one imperative destination short of my goal. I can't dress it up any other way; to miss Abu Dhabi will be abject failure.

Heaped on top of the passport issue is the recurring theme of being dead broke. Money, which is to say credit, is beginning to look dire. I still have more than the $4 I was down to at LAX but I can see the pathway to zero growing anxiously shorter by the day. I could sell my car back home, which I'll likely have to do anyways, but the kick in the nuts there is I still owe more than what the damn thing is worth. I'd sell my car and still owe the bank a few grand.

I have $1,800 left and still need to fly home to renew my passport before heading back to Abu Dhabi for a full week. Applying for more credit is no longer an option; no lending institution short of the Russian mob would lend me money now, and even they would likely laugh at me at this point. Defeat is beginning to feel imminent.

My only hope is to tuck tail firmly between legs and write Etihad, hoping they'll agree to switch the flight. If I'm ever going to get to Abu Dhabi, I need to fly home now.

In my search for the cheapest one-way flight back to Toronto, I come across Icelandair, who offer a stopover of up to seven nights at no additional charge. But does Iceland have a Manchester City supporters club? I remember checking back in August to see if Reykjavik had a club and not finding one. My mistake, I'll later learn, was searching in English. Had I only searched *stuðningsmannafélagið á Íslandi*, I would have discovered the Icelandic Blues months earlier.

Not yet possessing this knowledge, I email Howard, desperately hoping he would know of a club I had somehow missed. He did. Howard writes back immediately, as he has done with every message I've sent him in the past two months. There is indeed an Icelandic branch and Howard quickly puts me in touch with them. The Iceland Blues write back just as quickly as Howard did and confirm that yes, they will be assembling in Reykjavik this Saturday for City's away match versus Hull.

Twenty-four hours after arriving back in Manchester from Gibraltar, I say a quick and teary goodbye to my sister and my brother-in-law, and set out on my penultimate flight.

15
REYKJAVIK

The Kings of Búland Street

I CAN recall with great clarity being in my high school library, curiously scouring through a computer CD of countries around the world, a sort of Wikipedia atlas, before Wikipedia – I even remember thinking I was on the internet and didn't quite get what all the fuss was about.

Like most 17-year-olds growing up in a suburb of less than 80,000 people, I had soured on my hometown and begun my search for someplace new and exciting. This CD atlas search somehow ended up on Iceland: 100% literacy rate, 2% unemployment and a scattering of proper hockey rinks. Iceland, to 17-year-old me, sounded like heaven on Earth, and I quickly decided the capital city of Reykjavik was where I would move.

In the weeks that followed, I came to accept just how implausible a move to Iceland is for a Canadian teenager without a job – or perhaps I simply lost interest. My dream of moving to Iceland remained just that and instead I decided to quit school and take a night-shift job loading trucks at my best friend's family business.

Iceland became just another word, soon to slip into the recesses of something I once believed might be a good idea. Seventeen-year-old me wouldn't be too enamoured with his current-day self: 20 years older, broke and still having never seen Iceland.

Twenty years of waiting comes to an end at 12.25pm as the fog lifts and Icelandair flight FI441 goes wheels up and banks northwest towards Keflavik. Icelandair's legroom in coach is easily that of business class on most other commercial carriers. The company also names their planes, and learning ours is called *Eldfjall* – which means volcano or 'Mountain of fire' in Icelandic – has me thinking of my friends Marc Luk and Peter Finch.

Over 100 Icelandic albums are featured on the seat-back entertainment and the inflight menu is written with a refreshing sense of humour:

Baguette – Long bread is more fun than shortbread. You can use it in many fun ways if you want. You could try balancing it on your nose or head, or even use it to poke your neighbour (only if you know them!). Or you can just eat it.

Olives – The healthy, versatile gem of the Mediterranean. What turns gin and vermouth into a martini. Also good for snacking.

Even on my flight there, I get the sense I am travelling to a place too small to worry about red tape and how the rest of the world does things. Islands almost always march to their own beat, and I am jumping out of my seat with the notion of discovering Iceland's rhythm.

The film list on Icelandair's inflight personal entertainment tablet is second to none. *Zodiac, Before Sunset, The Color Purple, Garden State, L.A. Confidential, Magnolia, Reykjavik Rotterdam* (which is the original *Contraband*), *Annie Hall, Little Miss Sunshine* and *Singing in the Rain*. And that's just naming a fraction of the impressive titles. How often in life do we judge people based on their favourite films, music, or sports teams? If this can be any sort of gauge, Reykjavik is going to surpass even my wildest high school expectations. Twenty years after I first dreamed of it, I finally touch down in Iceland.

There is no line when I arrive at customs, just two border guards, both of whom resemble taller and equally handsome Matt Damons. I tell myself it's a good thing I'm not single and living in Reykjavik, as competing for women against my first impression of Icelandic men would be an uphill battle, to say the least. I take a moment, watching the two movie star lookalikes laugh and joke with one another before approaching.

'How long will you be staying in Iceland?' Damon #1 asks.

'Just for the weekend.'

'Just a stopover on your way home to Toronto?'

'Yes,' I answer.

And that word home sounds good. A weekend in Reykjavik, then home.

I clear customs to find a waiting man in his early-50s, wearing a City scarf wrapped around his neck, a dead ringer for Brian Dennehy. This is Tómas Hallgrimsson. Tommi, as I will come to know him, will be my host for the weekend and of all the incredible hosts I've enjoyed along this journey, he will be the one I spend the most time with. Tommi is no stranger to entertaining and the 40-minute drive from Keflavik to Reykjavik feels much shorter.

'Looks like *Star Trek*,' Tommi says, sensing my fascination with the passing landscape.

'It's like nothing I've ever seen before,' I reply.

Tommi's comparison, though odd, is strangely accurate. The volcanic rocks, which have formed much of the landscape, look more like the surface of the moon than anything I've seen here on Earth.

'You remember the volcanoes going off in Iceland a few years ago, the ones that disrupted flights all around the world?' Tommi asks in perfect English, his accent causing my native language to sound both eloquent and endearing at the same time.

'Of course.'

'Well, did you know the only airlines that kept flying were the Icelandic domestic ones? We are used to it, you see!'

It's a strange point of pride and I don't know why I mention it here. Perhaps it is because I too am from a country that carries curious points of pride and I appreciate the national oddities we hold dear.

Tommi is unable to hang out this evening, a work dinner having been scheduled weeks in advance. It's no bother to me. My hotel is directly in the heart of Reykjavik and I'm happy to go exploring. Tommi drops me off at the hotel Centrum in the heart of downtown Reykjavik and we agree to meet on this spot tomorrow morning.

My first mission is to find food. I promised myself I would have at least one fancy seafood dish somewhere along this journey and Reykjavik seems as good a place as any to follow through on that promise. I quickly learn however that Iceland is way out of my price range, a simple order of fish and chips pushing $20 Canadian, meaning anything more gourmet is categorically out of the question.

I settle for a sandwich shop across from my hotel called Hlölla Bátar and decide on something called the *hrekkjusvin*, which judging from the cartoon picture of a pig, is some sort of pulled pork. Maybe it is just because I am so hungry, but the *hrekkjusvin* – which oddly translates to 'bullies' – with its perfect balance of mayo, fat, and dripping barbecue sauce, may just be the most delicious thing I've had this season.

After take-away sandwich bliss, I head up Laugavegur street, dotted with pubs, small art galleries, and souvenir shops selling those iconic sweaters knitted from Icelandic sheep's wool. I used to think these sweaters were a touch lame, but seeing them in every shop window, in the environment they were made for, I suddenly want one as badly as I've ever wanted any material item. But at 20,000 Icelandic Krona, or $180 Canadian, it will have to wait until next time.

The most curious and charming sight I stumble across on day one is a wrought iron fence, whose spears are tipped with individual mittens and a sign in English that reads, 'Single gloves speed dating'. A place too small to worry how the rest of the world does things? Absolutely.

Next morning, Tommi picks me up in front of the hotel, and his slightly grey appearance suggests he may be feeling the effects of a work dinner that went late into the evening. We wind our way through Reykjavik's narrow downtown streets, the grey and barren trees of March and light dusting of snow very much resembling the place where I grew up. We arrive about five minutes later – all things being relatively close in the small city of just under 200,000 – at Vox, a gourmet restaurant in the Hilton, the home to Iceland's most popular brunch buffet. As I walk past endless rows of Icelandic and Western fusion I am certain this brunch will spell the end of my money. If I couldn't afford fish and chips, I'd have to sell a kidney for this fare.

The four dessert tables are bigger than most buffets I've ever seen – and I grew up in North America – and only serve to complement the miles of food that stretch the length of the restaurant, ending as you arrive at your own personal omelette chef. I take advantage of the miniature eggs Benedict before getting a little more adventurous with some Icelandic fish, made less adventurous by my slathering of hollandaise sauce. And as we're off to a footy match, I simply can't resist the offering of a British fry-up: sausage, bacon, beans, repeat.

As Tommi and I chat over multiple plates of brunch – his looking far more colourful and local than mine – I ask him if he's ever heard the story of the 1920 Winnipeg Falcons.

'The what?' he asks.

'The Falcons!' I reply incredulously. 'They were a team made up almost entirely of Icelandic immigrants, who won the first Olympic gold medal in ice hockey.'

For a proud Icelander such as Tommi, this revelation of quasi-Icelandic triumph has caused his eyes to nearly separate from their sockets.

'Are you sure?' he asks.

'Of course I'm sure, here look.'

I take out my phone and pull up the Wikipedia page, scrolling to the section with a list of player names, before passing it to Tommi.

'Haldor Halderson! This is an Icelandic name!' he says. Tommi's voice grows louder and more excited with each name thereafter, 'Konrad Johannesson! Look, the coach was called Gordon Sigurjonson. This is truly amazing,' Tommi says, handing back my phone as he heads for the dessert trays.

After our tiny plates are filled to the edges with crème brûlée, small cakes of chocolate and lemon, and mounds of fresh fruit – I don't even want to guess at the price of fresh fruit salad in Iceland – Tommi, as so many of my saving-grace hosts have on this journey, picks up the entire tab, which I can only imagine is significantly north of any sum I have ever paid in a restaurant.

As we drive from Vox towards the pub, our bellies full, I notice Tommi tends to hum during breaks in the conversation. There are no words, rather an almost intrinsic marching rhythm and burred r's, 'Prrrummmp pup, pup, brum pup pup pup.' I doubt he even knows he's doing it, simply a man at peace after a good night, a gourmet brunch and a match about to begin.

Laugardagur, 15. mars. Hull City gegn City. Leikurinn hefst kl. 12.45

Tommi and I pull into the underground parking lot, just beside Ölver Sportbar – Álfheimum 74, 104 Reykjavik – for a crucial away match versus Hull. Ölver is a large four-room single-level pub on the outskirts of the city. It was the first real sports pub in Reykjavik and if its wide array of scarves and memorabilia from every club from Derby County to Leeds doesn't convince me this is the spot to watch English football, the Leyton Orient versus Brentford match playing on a small screens offers a measure of certainty.

I've certainly arrived in Reykjavik's Premier League headquarters. As I take in more of the surroundings a scarf catches my eye. It reads, 'Iceland v Croatia World Cup playoff 2013' and hangs proudly above the doorway; a reminder of just how close this small, isolated nation of

300,000 people came to qualifying for the world's biggest stage.

'We usually gather in the smaller room over there,' Tommi says, pointing to the smallest of the four rooms. 'We call it City Hall. But our match is on the big screen today so we'll be here in the main room,' he says with great pride.

I'm quickly introduced to Tommi's gang, beginning with the Iceland Blue's chairman Magnus Ingvason, or Maggi, which Tommi pronounces 'Mah-key', low on the 'Mah' then up on the 'key'.

Ludvik Birgisson, or 'Lulli', sits next to Maggi and rolls out their 2013/14 official supporters club pennant sent over from City, placing it on a custom stand they've built to rest on top of the table. All three men wear their ages well and Maggi, despite being the eldest, looks the youngest of the gang.

Tommi brings me over my first taste of Icelandic beer, which – due to a reason no one can seem to offer me – unlike other alcohols, was illegal in Iceland until 1989. As such the Icelanders have a little catching up to do in the beer department, the local beer wars dominated by two brands: Gull (which means Gold) and Viking (which means Viking). Tommi starts me off with Viking's take on a micro-brew, called Páska Bock, which at 6.7% is a stiff post-brunch lager.

With a cold beer in my hand and kick-off still a few minutes away, I ask the question that by now has become almost reflex.

'How did you boys get into City?'

'Maggi, Lulli and I have been City since 1968,' Tommi begins.

This answer grabs my full attention. It is fairly safe to say that the majority of the international Blues who aren't expats discovered City sometime between the early 1990s and now. Whether it be by way of Oasis, or Gillingham, Jimmy Grimble, or our 2012 miracle win, there aren't too many I've met who remember City lifting a trophy pre-2011.

'When we were children, we used to watch English football from the BBC, but one week after the matches had been played. The matches were always in black and white and we didn't know which team was which. One day, my father returned from a work trip to London and he brought me and my twin brother Thorir back a shirt each.'

Tommi holds his arms out as though he were his father holding up the two shirts.

'My father had a Liverpool shirt in one hand and City in the other. This was 1968 and they were the two most popular teams. My father said, "Tommi you can choose first." And of course I chose blue, because every kid knew red was a female colour.'

Ah, the bizarre stereotypes of a five-year-old growing up in 1960s Iceland.

'And does your brother still follow Liverpool?' I ask.

'Oh yes! He'll never change.'

Five-year-old Tommi managed to convince seven-year-old Maggi and six-year-old Lulli that red was a girl's colour, so they joined him on the good side of the battle and have been Blues for 45 years since.

'We all named our goldfish after City players, too,' Tommi says.

City has been knocked out of two competitions in the past week; 'A vexing seven days,' as my fellow City writer Mark Booth wrote so articulately in his pre-match piece. The Champions League exit to Barcelona and a shocking home defeat against Wigan have my City jinx seemingly in full effect, as I was actually in attendance for the FA Cup debacle. Howard Burr sat beside me at the match and put a humorous spin on the full-time whistle by declaring, 'At least I don't need to book any more coaches to Wembley this year.'

City versus Hull – a match I quickly realize will be called completely in Icelandic – kicks off at 12.45pm Greenwich Mean Time. If Icelandic in regular conversation sounds charmingly laid-back and pleasant, when shouted in unison by a pub full of Blues it is, by contrast, rather intense. There is a true guttural quality to Icelandic when one feels the need to shout.

A penalty not given is, *'Víti!'*

Desperate for your player to shoot? Cry out *'Skjóta!'*

And of course no football fan in any language can do without the Mozart cantata of swear words, *'Andskotinn!'* (Fuck!)

Shock arrives early to Ölver, when in the tenth minute, Vincent Kompany is stripped of the ball and hauls down Nikica Jelavic on a clear break. It's a rare misstep from our captain, but an unquestionable red card that could spell disaster for City's title hopes.

Our captain and defensive stalwart is off, furiously kicking a wall as he disappears down the KC Stadium tunnel. We're down to ten men and on the road against an on-form Hull City. *Andskotinn!*

All but one of the Reykjavik Blues is a born-and-raised Icelander. The other, Valmar Valjaots, is Estonian and plays the church pipe organ 240 miles northeast in Akureyri, 'Blue Moon' his particular favourite as the congregation exits. Not a single expat on the Iceland Blues roster, a record I haven't found and won't find anywhere else on my search.

'This is my therapy,' Tommi says, scanning the room of faces he's known his entire life. 'Men don't talk about our feelings, so we come here to talk about things and let it all out.'

Maybe this is just a divorced father of two's take on things, or perhaps this is an Icelandic thing. Are Icelanders notoriously closed off? Do they not discuss their feelings as openly as other cultures?

I've heard similar stereotypes about Ireland and Scandinavia, which I don't particularly buy into, after all how could this be true of places that produced James Joyce or The Cardigans?

And the music to come out of Iceland is the most emotive I've ever heard. Perhaps that's just it. Perhaps the way Icelanders discuss their feelings is less direct. It's in the songs they compose, the vibrancy of the paint they choose to coat their buildings in, or the way they shout at a television screen flashing images from another island not so far away anymore. Or perhaps Tommi is right, maybe men here simply, 'don't discuss their feelings'. Maybe red is a feminine colour.

Within minutes of Kompany's sending-off – minutes that feel like hours – David Silva hits one from 20 yards out, curling it narrowly inside the post. A deep Viking roar ripples through the bar, and I imagine us all on a rickety wooden ship invading the shores of Newfoundland. We're up 1-0 heading into the half with a belief we might just be able to steal these three points.

I head to the bar for another bottle of Viking and in the background I can overhear Tommi telling Maggi about our morning.

'Have you heard this story?' Tommi asks.

'Yes, there was a story in the paper a few years ago,' Maggi answers.

'But listen to the names, Sigurjonson, Halderson, all Icelanders!'

Maggi, the patriarchal figure of the three friends, is impressed but more reserved, almost the way an older brother entertains the story of his younger sibling. It is obvious to me after just half a match of football that they share a very long, very beautiful friendship.

In the 70th minute, with Hull on the attack, City about to make a change, and the season hanging in the balance, I ask Maggi if he'd make any changes.

'I'd bring on Milner,' he replies.

I am inclined to agree, but Pellegrini instead brings on Lescott. It isn't until the 89th minute that Edin Dzeko – after a classic miss just minutes earlier – puts us two goals to the good, finishing a sublime ball from the clear man of the match, David Silva. A few minutes later, the final whistle blows on a huge away win for City. If we do end up winning the league, this might well be a performance we look back on as the difference maker.

The Iceland Blues assemble for a quick group photo, as I pass Maggi my notebook and ask if he could write down their names from left to right.

On 14 March 2013, nearly 20 years after I first dreamed of this place, the following Blues joined me in a bar in Reykjavik to watch a Manchester City football match. Haraldur, Haraldur, Boas, Hallur, Tommi, Thorri, Hallgrimur, Magnus, Sigurjon, Freyja, Herbert, Throstur, Ludvik, Aron, Vidar.

Reykjavík

As Tommi drives me back to the hotel, he once again apologizes a work dinner means he will again be unable to hang-out. I assure him it is fine, as by complete coincidence, I have a Canadian friend in town and we have plans to hit some place called Lebowski Bar.

A few hours later, at a *Big Lebowski*-themed bar in Reykjavik, my friend Carly and I drink pints of Gull, and laugh, and fall into that blissful patter of obscure references appreciated only by those born in the same year and region of the world. The Coen brothers on this occasion, as they more often do, serve to elevate my spirits from heights that were already lofty, and I can't imagine a more perfect evening.

The following morning, I check out of my hotel and throw my bags one last time into the back of Tommi's Nissan. We grab some midday pizza at the local mall, and on our way out have a chance encounter with two members of the Icelandic women's ice hockey team. The girls are setting up a fundraiser and proudly show me their team jersey, the logo featuring a falcon with a small maple leaf.

'What's the red maple leaf for?' I ask.

'It acknowledges the 1920 Falcons. They won the first-ever Olympic gold medal. Have you heard of them?'

Tommi quickly interjects, 'Of course, they were all Icelanders!'

Before leaving, the girls tell us there is a big club match on in Reykjavik tonight, the second game of the men's finals, and we assure them we will be in attendance.

We return to Ölver bar and watch United versus Liverpool, with Lulli and Maggi. The pub is overflowing, five or six times the attendance of yesterday, the two largest rooms serving to separate Scouse red from Trafford red. City still have a way to come to be top draw in Iceland, but it's a title I don't think Tommi and his gang are too worried about.

Again I offer to buy Tommi a beer, as he picked up the lunch tab. Another work dinner gone late into the Icelandic night, Tommi finally confesses, 'I think I'm marinated.'

We have a tough time deciding who to pull for; we need Liverpool to lose to increase our title hopes, but United, who are enduring their worst campaign in decades, are still too classic a foe, and we decide we'll support Liverpool in this one, and win the title from them later on, without help from you-know-who.

After Liverpool dispatch our bitter, grunting rivals – and in doing so retain top spot in the league – Tommi drives me around every square inch of Reykjavik. We visit the famous church called Hallgrímskirkja, Reykjavik's tallest structure, which from the top provides a spectacular view of the town below, thousands of little brightly coloured buildings, bursting in loud contrast to their drab winter canvas. Next we head to the lesser-known Perlan building that, from its 360-degree observation deck, offers an even more fantastic panoramic view of Reykjavik. A strong wind kicks up and I watch as a storm arrives in seconds from over the North Atlantic, before dashing back into the revolving restaurant for cover.

Down on the waterfront, Tommi shows me where he and his brother celebrated their 50th birthday last year.

'We surprised all the guests and arrived by boat.'

Today's late game is Tottenham versus Arsenal, and Tommi asks if I'd like to watch it at his place. I say of course and he tells me he just needs to make a stop first. We pull into a lonely strip plaza; the four small units are as grey as the day surrounding them. The butcher is next to the baker and I watch from the car as Tommi quickly darts from one to the other.

Back at Tommi's modest apartment that he shares with his youngest City-supporting son, Styrmir – his other son, Valgeir, supports the red part of Manchester, poor Tommi – Tommi introduces me to his wall of fame, framed pictures of him with just about any City legend you can name from Colin Bell, to Shaun Goater, Paul Lake to Benjani. Even legendary kit man Les Chapman has a spot in Tommi's shrine.

One picture seems to hold a more prominent spot on the wall than any of the others, the centerpiece of the collage. This spot is held by late-'60s and early-'70s Manchester City icon Francis Lee.

Franny Lee, the City favourite who helped the lads in sky blue lift a league title in 1968 and then, in 1969, an FA Cup title – his club this time dressed in brilliant bars of black and red. Francis Lee who was sold to Derby County and got so angry he helped them win the league in his first season. Francis Lee who got so angry he punched out Norman Hunter right on the pitch. Francis Lee who went on to make a small fortune in toilet roll. Francis Lee who holds centre-spot on Tommi Hallgrimsson's living room wall, in Reykjavik.

Tommi next parades his collection of Manchester City jerseys from over the years, a collection that stretches back decades and features all the colours of the City rainbow in a folded pile at least a metre high. After the brief fashion show he disappears into the kitchen before reemerging with endless plates of local meats and cheeses, pastries and cups of tea.

I've travelled the entire world, stayed in some incredible places and eaten some delicious (and not-so-delicious) food, but here in Iceland, in this moment, eating meats from the local butcher and pastries from the local baker, watching football after our team has got the job done for the week, listening to a father and son discuss things in Icelandic, which I don't for a moment pretend to understand, but imagine have to do with the performance of Tottenham's Icelandic native son, Gylfi Sigurdsson – this is the room, the time, the place, the food, the company, the one moment, I could return to over and over again and never tire of.

After watching Arsenal defeat their London rivals, Tommi has a surprise for me on our way to watch the hockey. We pull into a tiny side street a block or two from his current apartment. We get out and he points to the street sign, Búland Gata.

'This is it. This is where we grew up.'

Búland is a tidy little street made up of small single- and two-storey homes, shades of white only slightly duller than the snow on their doorsteps. Tommi points to a small patch of grass peeking through the snow at the end of the street.

'Each street had a football team made up of children from that street. Búland Street was called The Falcons and that patch was our home pitch. We called it Wembley.'

'Were Maggi and Lulli on the team?' I ask.

'Yes! Maggi was Rodney Marsh and Lulli was always Colin Bell.'

'Who were you?'

Tommi's eyes return to the late '60s and in his mind, I know he sees Búland Street and Wembley exactly as they were. His sky-blue Falcons taking on a neighbouring street wearing red. Maggi, the captain, delivering the ball to Lulli, sending him on a fierce run down the wing. Lulli then floats a cross into Tommi who just manages to get his forehead on to the ball, directing it past the keeper and in between two balled-up jackets used as goal posts.

'I was Francis Lee, of course.'

Tommi can point to nearly every house on the block, and tell you not only the names of the families who lived there, but also which club they supported.

'Maggi's mom used to watch us from that window over there. She once told me she watched while Maggi made me and Lulli form a wall so he could smash the ball into us. I remember that day, it really hurt!'

Before heading off, Tommi takes in one last exaggerated breath of Búland Street air.

'Does anything feel better than coming home?' he asks.

'I'll let you know tomorrow,' I reply.

16
ABU DHABI

Added Time

THE DAY of 1 September 2008 was one that would transform not just a club, but an entire community. That morning, Manchester, and the world for that matter, awoke to the news that overnight City's embattled and controversial owner had sold their beloved Blues to someone or something called the Abu Dhabi United Group. The news that their club had, overnight, become one of if not the richest in football could easily have been the biggest news of a generation, but it was not even the biggest news of that day for City.

Within hours of the purchase and mere moments away from the transfer deadline, Sheikh Mansour and his ownership group wanted to show their new fans and the football world just how serious they were. Only hours before the transfer deadline, City swooped in and landed Brazilian superstar Robinho even though the football world and indeed Chelsea themselves were convinced a deal to Stamford Bridge was all but complete. Perennial minnows Manchester City had landed the biggest prize of the transfer window sweepstakes, the club who once struggled to pay for paint to mark the lines on the pitch shelling out a then-record £32.5m. Overnight there was a new competitor in world football, they wore sky blue and came from the east of Manchester. The club's fortunes, its global reach and the lives of the citizens of Manchester were about to change in a big way.

City's new owners released a statement that day, which I believe – given the frequent emptiness of such promises – merits revisiting:

> 'We in Abu Dhabi United Company for Development and Investment are keen to develop ways to provide support and care for various sports activities to help build and develop a new generation… which represents the real wealth and the future of this nation and the cornerstone for building the future of our civilization. As embodied in our mission to open new horizons in all kinds of sports, it will enable them to enjoy healthy body and mind, thanks to the lessons we have learned from the wise leadership in Abu Dhabi.
>
> 'We will adopt marketing plans that reflect positively on the club and the company from investments in all sectors of television marketing and purchasing of star player, as well as development of infrastructure facilities at the club.'

Rarely have the bold words of new ownership ever been so well lived up to. Five years later, an FA Cup and Premier League title are not the only remarkable accomplishments for Sheik Mansour and his ownership group. City's triumphs on the pitch are a fraction of the club's influence off it.

The Etihad Campus, which includes a sixth form college, new community football pitches and myriad sport facilities have generated thousands of new jobs in an area of Manchester that desperately needed them.

So, given our owner from Abu Dhabi's impact on Manchester, how could I possibly attempt a book such as this without a visit to the place that helped change the fortunes of City? I suppose there is, of course, the small matter of getting there.

Curse this expiring passport and its photo of a noticeably younger man staring back at me and hurling insults at its aged holder: Stupid! Broke! Useless!

It wasn't anyone at Manchester City who first put me in touch with Etihad, nor any of the many well-connected Blues I've met along the way. In the end, it was my friend and former business partner Chris Reilly, the man whose quasi-firing of me kick-started this entire journey. Chris, another man who genuinely knows everyone – a sort of Tim Bramley of Newmarket, if you will – has a Jamaican friend named Rohan Foster. Rohan is a pilot for, you guessed it, Etihad. Who would have imagined that Manchester City's principal partner and the airline belonging to the same ownership group had a senior pilot from Jamaica who splits his time between Abu Dhabi and Newmarket, Ontario? So that is how I was introduced to David Cook and offered a free flight from Manchester to Abu Dhabi, which I now have to turn down due to my expiring passport.

With my tail tucked quite firmly between my legs, I write David Cook – a man who had just helped finish a deal with Major League Soccer in North America and was working on another deal with Formula 1 – the most unprofessional email he has likely ever received.

David and Etihad could have simply replied, 'You're an idiot, mate, that's the best we can do. Sorry you're so dumb, good luck in your futile search for intelligence.'

Luckily David is someone who understands these things happen in life and just before I boarded my plane from Reykjavik to Toronto I received an email which read, 'Get home, renew your passport and we'll get you over to Abu Dhabi from Toronto.'

Racing home for five days was a minor disaster. I had to hope the Canadian Ministry of Citizenship and Immigration – not always known for its swiftness – was going to rush renew my passport as they claimed was possible, as long as I could prove my need for renewal was urgent, usually by providing proof of imminent flight. But I was still without a tangible ticket as evidence of impending travel.

The latest I could leave things was Wednesday, which I did. On Wednesday morning I set out to the passport office without a ticket, just emails from Etihad hoping that might do the trick.

Just as I was locking my front door my phone chimed, signalling a new email, 'Darryl, sorry for the late reply, please find attached your ticket to Abu Dhabi… departing Saturday morning.'

Ho-ly shit. I literally have 48 hours to get this passport renewed and jump on a Boeing 777 bound for the Middle East. Passport Canada, don't fail me now.

Sure enough my country comes through for me, and by Friday at noon I hold my shiny new ten-year passport. I took pictures of all 26 pages in my old document, all the stamps from this journey, places I'd never imagined going, and some I'd never even heard of before this year. Armed with my new ten-year version, I catch myself wondering which stamps might paint the next decade of these pages. The only thing I know for sure is the stamp for the Emirate of Abu Dhabi will be its first.

If all of this sounds difficult, it was afternoon tea compared to telling Jess that after only five days home, I was leaving again. I can't know it now, but the apartment we share together will have one less tenant when I finally return. Maybe a year away from home was always going to be too long for an already strained relationship. Or perhaps I didn't listen carefully enough to Glynn's advice back in Alkrington.

For now, a journey whose first stop was a two-mile drive east will conclude with a 12-hour flight in the same direction. My dad gives me a lift to the airport and we joke along the way about the prospect of me not having a beer for a week, such is our ignorance regarding my destination.

Icelandair was nice – really nice! But flying Etihad is another world entirely. Even in coach, you're given proper silverware with the Etihad logo engraved in each handle, you can watch live Premier League games on your personal seat-back television (let me say this again just to be clear: at 35,000 feet I watched *live* Premier League football). Etihad, it is safe to say, is like nothing I have ever experienced. I'm sure the knowledge that they are sponsoring this flight might create a perceived notion of bias, so with that in mind, let me just hit you with this – vegetable curry for lunch and lamb for dinner. Biased, my ass – City has the best airline in the land and all the world, full stop. It's not a plane, it is a hotel that can fly. A seat aboard Etihad is better than most apartments I've lived in.

As we float peacefully over the North Atlantic, I select City's 4-1 destruction of United from the archived match menu in my seat-back entertainment. As the match plays, around about the spot when Sergio put us up by three goals, I close my eyes and fall away back to Chicago where I first watched this match. The breeze through a rolled-down cab window returns, and I can hear Mark Zanatta and Andrew Tripp arguing about bagels in the background, as the serene memory gently tucks me into a deep slumber. When my eyes open again, I'm over the desert, approaching the shores of the Persian Gulf, many miles from home.

My visit to the Emirate of Abu Dhabi – one of seven Emirates that together form the country of United Arab Emirates – will be six days long and I will call Yas Island home for the duration. Yas Island is ten miles from the airport and another 12 from downtown.

My cab driver – a Nepalese gentleman with an intense love of Bryan Adams – tells me Yas Island didn't exist ten years ago. The island – which is man-made – was designed as a tourist oasis and a home to Abu Dhabi's crown sporting jewel, the F1 race at Yas Marina Circuit.

When the F1 isn't in town, which is 51 weeks of the year, the rates here are extremely reasonable; my hotel room, four stars, with a pool and a gym, goes for about £60 per night. During the F1 festivities, this price more than quintuples.

I arrive in Abu Dhabi in the early evening and it doesn't take long to find my first drink. I'd read on the government of Canada's travel advisory page that alcohol can be a tricky issue in the UAE, but if I was slightly worried I might arrive to discover a dry state, I needn't have been. Expat Darren Ball, chairman of the Abu Dhabi Blues – who unfortunately has to fly out of town for business ahead of the derby – has suggested we meet for a beer at the hotel next to mine. I walk next door to one of the six hotels of varying affluence all neatly arranged around a giant cul-de-sac to find Darren with his wife, Gaynor, the attractive couple in their late 30s already enjoying tall pints of Peroni.

'So tell me the alcohol situation here, are we okay to have a few?' I ask.

'Absolutely, bars here are the same as anywhere, the only difference being they are limited to the hotels; you won't find a pub in the way you would back home,' Darren tells me, after sipping a pint that looks somehow larger than in other countries. 'You also don't want to be publicly drunk, that's a big one. But if you limit your drinking to the hotel bars and your home, you're absolutely fine.'

'Are you ready for your free drinks sir?' the waiter asks Darren.

'Not just yet, mate, we'll let you know,' he replies.

'Did I hear him right?' I ask.

'Yeah, drinks here are buy-one-get-one-free on your first orders.' So much for not getting a drink in Abu Dhabi.

Darren Ball's mom was a Red but Darren, a lifelong Blue, chose to follow along patriarchal bloodlines as have his sons Declan and Aidan. Gaynor, a Red, married Darren on 13 May 1995 and one can only imagine what it was like celebrating their 17th anniversary against the backdrop of the most thrilling Premier League finish in history.

After a few pints and some unexpected ice hockey talk – the well-travelled Balls used to live in New Jersey during the Devils' heyday – we head across the complex to another bar and meet an old friend of Darren's who has come to Abu Dhabi to help coach football clinics for the week as part of the City In The Community initiative.

By sheer coincidence, this is also one of the coaches I am to be following around this week, as per my agreement with David Cook and Etihad. Eight hours ahead of schedule, I meet Paul Kelly, or PK as he is better known, for a late-night chalice of Stella, and another, before having just one more.

The next morning I pull on a white golf shirt with the City and Etihad logo, given to me somewhat prophetically by Danny Reynolds.

Looking as professional as a man with jet lag as well as Stella-lag can at 7.30am, I drag my feet the few hundred metres over to the Radisson Blu Hotel where PK and the other coaches are staying.

PK jumps on our minibus fresh as a daisy, as though Stella were simply vitamin water. Joined by PK are Sinead Quinn, who is with Etihad and is helping arrange my visit, and three other coaches, Hannah Steele, Craig Bell and Mike Dixon.

Our drive into the city provides my first real glimpse of Abu Dhabi. The entire underpass of one of the highways is a gorgeous tiled mosaic of galloping horses, absorbing shades of beige, yellow and sky blue. I marvel at the majestic Sheikh Zayed Mosque – named for the forefather of this relatively new country – shining in the distance with its marble and mother of pearl exterior. In 30 minutes of driving I see countless lavish homes along the roadways and scarcely a shit car in sight – Abu Dhabi presenting a staggering ratio of sweet rides to beaters.

We pull into the Centre For Disabilities some time around 8.30am just as the last of the children are arriving. 'Look, he's got a City top on!' PK points out proudly, regarding a late arrival whose dad has just wished him a good day.

Before I was a writer, or much of a musician, or even an assistant manager at a sports shop, I worked teaching sports to adults with physical and mental disabilities. Going back even further than that to my earliest memories, I can recall my Aunt Gracie who, in a life that would become filled with innumerable friendships, was my very first friend in this world.

Gracie had Down's syndrome along with a heart defect that meant doctors didn't expect her to survive longer than a few years. But as so many people with disabilities do, Gracie fought the odds and surprised us all, living a full and rich 21 years, inspiring everyone fortunate enough to have met her.

As we walk into the Centre For Disabilities, I am as excited as I have been at any juncture in the past year. I don't feel qualified as a writer, certainly not as a journalist; sometimes I feel as though I've blagged my way through this entire adventure. But here, at this school, I know I'm in a world I recognize and adore – a world in which outsiders think the more fortunate are helping the less fortunate, when in fact reality is quite the opposite.

Before the students arrive, I help the coaches set up and manage to only slightly embarrass myself in a game of keepie-uppie.

'Look at me, I'm an elephant,' Paul yells, swaying his right arm in front of his face. PK, a former bricklayer from Wythenshawe who decided to reinvent his career three years ago, marches the group of about 50 children around a terrific gymnasium. As the children chase PK around doing their best impressions of elephants, I can't help but imagine Manuel Pellegrini running this drill with the first team.

The students switch from animal to animal at PK's command, never taking their eyes off him, hanging on his every word. When Paul shouts, 'Lion!' the children marvel at the skills of Mike Dixon, the former amateur boxer from Denton, now gracefully portraying the king of the jungle.

After a fabulous session of role-play and ball handling drills turned into team games, Hannah guides the young pupils in the ways of the penalty kick. One by one the students line up and blast goals past Craig, the ultra-athletic footballer perhaps easing up a bit on his dives left and right.

After the session we're invited into an adjacent room where our hosts have put out an attractive spread of pastries and tea served in china cups. I speak with some of the faculty and let them know how impressed I am with the centre. You can always tell when children with disabilities are well looked after, it comes through in their enthusiasm, the brightness in their eyes and the smiles on their faces.

Today I didn't see one child with anything but a wide and brilliant grin, which from my experience would speak both to the educators here at the centre as well as a supportive family at home. It is only a small glimpse into how people with disabilities are cared for in Abu Dhabi, but from what I witnessed today, the Emirate and its Centre For Disabilities are to be commended. And from my observations of PK and his crew, the citizens of Manchester can be proud in the knowledge that this gang's work back home is being spread around the globe.

I haven't thought of my Aunt Gracie in a long time – too long. My parting thought as we leave the centre is of her and of how much she would have loved today.

.س‌رام 25 ءاثالثلا 23:45 ةعاسلا ، يتيس x دتيانوي

A 30-minute taxi ride that cost me all of about $20 concludes at the NRG bar, in Le Méridien Hotel, 10th St, Abu Dhabi, United Arab Emirates. The Abu Dhabi downtown isn't quite the spectacle Dubai is, and it is a far shout from what I experienced in Hong Kong. Still, with one million people in a city that was scarcely 60,000 just

30 years ago, one gets the impression this might be where Abu Dhabi is headed. The Méridien is – like most things here – modern, luxurious and Western.

Through the lavish entrance and to my right, I discover NRG bar, its waft of cigarette smoke greeting me long before my first step inside. Darren had given me the heads-up that a match on a Tuesday at midnight could be a tough sell in Abu Dhabi, even if it is the derby. Work contracts here can be strict when it comes to midweek drinking and most expats prefer to leave any indulgences for the weekend. Darren assured me there would be at least one Blue worth the trip, 'Go see Marchy, he's all you'll need for a good time.'

As I approach NRG's long and winding bar, I can only see one City top, worn by an older gentleman who doesn't strike me as a wild man. I want to order a pint before introducing myself, but the selection of typical import lagers doesn't pique my interest, so I make my way to the end of the bar, empty-handed and thirsty to meet this man in blue.

'Are you Marchy?' I ask.

'No, I'm Paul,' he replies, confused by the 'American' carrying a notebook and wearing a City scarf.

Paul Kerr, in his early 60s, a born-and-bred Mancunian Blue, has traversed more of this world than I could in a dozen books. His recent assignment, which not surprisingly is in the oil business, is here in Abu Dhabi – his daughter and son-in-law now working here as well. Paul and I chat a few minutes longer before a man armed with two pints of Kilkenny and a Manchester City scarf strides purposefully in our direction. The approaching man looks like a slightly older, but more tanned and more intimidating Jimi Goodwin from the band Doves, and I know instantly that this must be the one they call Marchy.

'*You* must be Marchy,' I say, extending my hand. 'Where did you find Kilkenny?'

Marchy puts down one of his pints and shakes my hand.

'The Irish pub at the other side of the hotel, I'll go get you one, mate.'

Before I can say, 'It's no trouble,' Marchy is off to the neighbouring hotel's pub. He returns with a Kilkenny for me and two more for himself, just as the second and final Manchester derby is about to kick off.

Every single chairman I reached out to this season wanted me to visit their club on derby day. It would be any club's best foot forward, a date that would guarantee a packed pub full of Blues in any city … everywhere except tonight in Abu Dhabi, that is.

'Shame you had to be here for a midweek derby, not many of us can get out so late on a weeknight,' Marchy says. And so it is that Paul Kerr, David Marchington, and Darryl Webster stand in a hotel bar in the United Arab Emirates at the stroke of midnight, a trio of anxious Blues ready to watch Manchester City kick off against our most bitter rivals.

We didn't have to wait long for a goal in Chicago and we've barely swallowed a sip of Irish ale before Samir Nasri streaks into the box, checks his shot, fakes Rio Ferdinand out of his boots and lets go a belter off the post. Edin Dzeko one-times the rebound home, silencing the Old Trafford faithful, and thousands of miles away in Abu Dhabi, three Blues who only met ten minutes earlier wrap one another in bear hugs and leap so high we almost knock our heads off the sports bar's overhanging second tier. City 1, United 0. The double is on!

The rest of the half is scoreless, and despite City looking dominant, the old Blue nerves are still out in full force.

Marchy slips out to the rival hotel bar and returns with a second-half supply of Kilkenny for the two of us.

Marchy introduces me to a local man named Omar, who was an Arsenal supporter until the day Sheikh Mansour purchased City. This brings about an important topic: switching clubs. For most, this notion of treason, even if it is to join their preferred side, is difficult to reconcile. But let's take a step back and have a think on this. For those fortunate enough to be born in Manchester, a small city with – allegiances aside for a moment – two world-class football clubs, the idea of having more than one club in your lifetime is simply unfathomable.

But I would like you to consider for a moment, life as a football supporter, growing up in a country – as I did – that didn't have a professional league anywhere near the same class as in Europe. What do you do when you grow up adoring football in a country without a strong domestic league? First you choose a league, usually the most televised one wins – this is usually England's Premier League (La Liga is close, having Barcelona and Real Madrid, but nothing rivals England in terms of international following). So you quickly fall in love with English Premier football.

But you've never been there and you have no family ties. Your only link is a satellite signal and flashing frames on a television, or a dodgy internet stream that has a special knack for freezing just as striker puts laces to ball. Where's the connection? Who will you support?

Perhaps it's a player you fall in love with: Francis Lee, George Best, Thierry Henry. Maybe a certain logo or colour speaks to you. You select your club and off you go. Until one day, a more powerful link, a completely unexpected tie enters your footballing life. Imagine the most revered man in your small country had a grandson who loved football the way you did. Now imagine this grandson purchased a team and splashed one of your words – ETIHAD – proudly across the front of the jersey for all the world to see. Every time this club scores, every time they lift a trophy, there it is, a link to your hometown. How could anyone in Abu Dhabi not jump ship for Manchester City? And how could anyone be vilified for doing so?

Would you give a hard time to a Canadian who once followed Rangers and Barcelona for becoming swept up in City culture after his sister moved to Manchester and mailed him home the most beautiful shirt his eyes had ever seen? I hope you wouldn't, just as I hope you wouldn't fault a man like Omar for making such a natural switch. Life is long enough to love many things; some people are born into that which they love, but for others, it takes some searching. Once you've found love you'll know it and the path that led you there should be mostly irrelevant.

Ten minutes into the restart, Samir Nasri and Edin Dzeko are at it again, the latter volleying the former's cross into the back of the net. The slow-motion replay demonstrates the incredible skill of our Bosnian striker, against a backdrop of crestfallen Reds watching through bars of twine, looking like prisoners in an inescapable hell. Winning at Old Trafford still feels slightly foreign to me, and the City nerves haven't quite subsided.

'Even if United pull two back, we'll still have a point from them at Old Trafford. Is that terrible to think?' I ask Marchy.

'No, mate, that's just City thinking,' he replies.

A Chelsea supporter at the table behind us tries kicking off with Marchy. The drinking laws are more relaxed than I expected, but one thing you certainly do *not* want over here is to be involved in any sort of bar brawl. Deportation at best, a few months in the can a real possibility. Marchy